Attune•ED
Mental Health Skills for Everyday Life
A Trauma-Informed Approach to Mental Health

Workbook 1: Self-Awareness

Lori Allen, PhD, MEd & Shin Shin Tang, PhD

Acknowledgments

We are deeply thankful that countless people have been part of our journey over the years in learning how to bring preventive mental health to workplaces. They include all of the education staff we have had the privilege of working with in various Oregon school districts, including Rainier, Fern Ridge, South Lane, 4J, Bethel, and Lane Educational Services District, and the Salem-Keizer Transportation Department.

In addition, we would like to thank all of our clients in our private practices who have shown us what it means to be resilient and courageous in the face of adversity. You were the original motivation to offer these skills and concepts to everyone.

Our editor, Tracy Ilene Miller, provided invaluable feedback and editing to help make this as accessible and concise as possible. Emily Peterson graciously offered her expertise in trauma and mental health to help make all aspects of our work practical. Mitzi Linn contributed to the beauty of the cover with her artwork. And finally, we would like to thank Emily, Ada Chester, Lela Ross, Matt Barnes, and Samantha Martínez for their support in bringing these skills and practices into the community with cultural humility and grace.

Attune•ED: Mental Health Skills for Everyday Life, A Trauma-Informed Approach to Mental Health, Workbook 1: Self Awareness

Cover & Book Design by Tracy Ilene Miller, millermarketingcomm@gmail.com
Cover Art, "Womantrees Dancing: Summertime," by Mitzi Linn

Contents

Mental Health in Everyday Life

Mental Health is a state of mental well-being that enables people to cope with the stresses of life . . . . It is an integral component of health and well-being that underpins our individual and collective abilities to make decisions, build relationships, and shape the world we live in. Mental health is a basic human right.
— World Health Organization[1]

Attuned: [2]

- To make receptive or aware

- To make harmonious

Attune•ED was developed to help create more harmony within and between people and the world around them.

Hi, and welcome to Attune•ED. Throughout this book, we hope you will learn new ways to attune to yourself and others. As mental health professionals and educators, we want to offer you practical, research-based concepts and skills that we see as foundational to mental health education.

Historically, mental health has focused primarily on mental illness, and mental health education and skills have been provided only when someone's mental health has become a problem. Instead, we see attending to mental health as a regular part of everyday life, just like physical health, bringing the potential for more daily joy, balance, and connection with others.

We all have intense emotions at times; being sad or anxious is a normal and often important part of life. However, not being able to manage these emotions in healthy ways contributes to chronic stress and illness, and impacts relationship building and day-to-day functioning. In fact, findings show that depression and anxiety predict poor future physical health as strongly as does smoking.[3]

Taking care of mental health involves a set of skills that can be learned and deepen with practice. In the same way that regular exercise can lower the risk of heart disease, regular maintenance of mental health can reduce the risk of anxiety and depression. Research has shown that we have more control over our mental health and wellbeing than previously thought, and that many mindfulness practices can actually help change the brain to increase physical and mental health.

Attune•ED teaches basic mental health concepts through a mindfulness lens in order to focus on health—and staying healthy—rather than focusing on pathology. The field of psychology offers decades of research on how to manage emotions effectively and the benefits of teaching behavioral skills. Attune•ED is unique in translating the most current and evidence-based psychological approaches into simple concepts and practices. In particular, the Attune•ED curriculum teaches core concepts from interpersonal neurobiology (IPNB), cognitive behavioral therapy (CBT), acceptance and commitment therapy (ACT), and dialectical behavioral therapy (DBT). It also incorporates evidence-based relationship and communication skills from The Gottman Institute as well as promising somatic therapy approaches.

In addition, Attune•ED emphasizes a mindfulness approach. Ancient Hindu and Buddhist texts describe many of the concepts and skills to maintain mental health that are now being researched and practiced in the West. Studies have shown that mindfulness helps reduce stress and increase wellbeing, including lower blood pressure and reduced burnout. Mindfulness can play an important role in countering the stress of everyday life and creating more calm internally and in relationships with others.

Stress & Trauma

Stress is an inevitable factor of life, and we need to distinguish between everyday stress and trauma. Some kinds of stress can be motivating and healthy, like the stress of a new experience that pushes physical and emotional boundaries. Running a marathon, taking a trip to a new country, or making a speech in front of 100 people can be stressful, but these events can also promote growth because they can push us right to, but not necessarily past, the point of being too overwhelmed to function. Soon after such an event, we most likely are able to return to a state of homeostasis, to a physical and emotional equilibrium. The key to being able to learn new information and emotional wellbeing is staying within this level of stress response.

> **Trauma is an event, or events, that causes long-term dysregulation in the nervous system.**[3]

Different than those temporary stressors, chronic stress, distress, and trauma are the types of stress that overwhelm physical and/or psychological resources, and trigger the nervous system into forms of fight, flight, freeze, or submit (FFFS) reactions. The result can be long-term dysregulation of the nervous system, which affects the nervous system's ability to respond flexibly to new stressors.[4] A person in this state might alternate between being avoidant and being flooded by reminders of the traumatic events. Under this kind of distress, rather than being in learning mode, survival mode takes over.

Research has shown a strong link between Adverse Childhood Experiences (ACEs) and physical and mental wellbeing.[5-7] ACEs are potentially traumatic or highly stressful events that occur to children, such as experiencing abuse or neglect, having a parent with a mental illness or addiction, and witnessing domestic violence. ACEs are remarkably common: Of American adults, 30 percent report having been abused as a child, and 20 percent, sexually abused. Not all children experience ACEs equally; income disparity and race are two of the greatest influences on risk for ACEs. Children from low-income families report greater numbers of ACEs than those from wealthy families, and Black, Asian, Native American, and Latinx children in the United States experience more ACEs than white children.[7-10]

The more ACEs one has experienced, the greater the likelihood of developing mental illness, substance abuse, and physical illnesses such as cancer and heart disease as an adult. Among children with ACEs, key areas of the brain responsible for long-term memory, problem solving, and emotional regulation are actually shrunken and have less neural connectivity than among children without ACEs. As a result, children with ACEs can have difficulty concentrating in school and remembering new information, and may exhibit acting-out behaviors.

In contrast, mindfulness-based mental health skills have been shown to reverse the effects of ACEs on the brain by promoting increased gray matter and neural connectivity.[11] Recent mindfulness studies among high-risk youth have demonstrated improvements in mental health symptoms, behavior, quality of life, and coping. Attune•ED's trauma-informed approach helps develop the ability to respond to difficult emotions with self-compassion and skill, rather than denial and shame. In this way, Attune•ED teaches you about mental health in ways similar to your learning about physical health—with information and tools to keep healthy.

However, for some individuals with a history of trauma, certain mindfulness practices such as sitting quietly or extending compassion toward others can actually increase anxiety. Therefore, we teach mindfulness and other coping strategies with care, in a manner that is sensitive to trauma. Throughout our curriculum, Attune•ED embeds trauma-informed theory, approaches, and practices.

It is important for us to distinguish between being trauma-informed and targeting symptoms of trauma. While Attune•ED can potentially help with some symptoms of trauma, that is not its focus. Rather, it is meant to be trauma-informed at a universal level to help you understand how to cope with stress and help you to know when to ask for additional help if you need it. At precisely what point stress should be regarded as "traumatic" is less important than understanding that your nervous system is dysregulated. Understanding stress and the body's stress response is the basis for creating and maintaining a healthy daily life.

Attune•ED is trauma-informed in the following ways:

1) **It emphasizes and establishes a foundation of getting to know oneself and how to regulate emotions before teaching relationship skills and interpersonal awareness.** Research indicates that individuals are more successful at applying relational skills when they are able to self-regulate.[12]

2) **It begins by teaching resourcing, or coping skills.** Specifically, using the emotional Window of Tolerance concept, you can begin to identify when you are getting agitated and introduce options for self-regulation that help keep you in your emotional Window of Tolerance.

3) **It provides alternative instructions for an individualized approach to mental health.** We invite you to participate in the experiential activities throughout the book—and also encourage discernment, because different practices work for different people and nervous systems, and some mindfulness activities can be counterindicated for people with trauma. Giving choices is a foundational trauma-informed approach that we deeply subscribe to and demonstrate in this Attune•ED workbook.

Better handling of emotions takes finding a balance between exposure to and avoidance of stress: Too much exposure to stress can lead to flooding the nervous system, and avoidance can exacerbate the problem. As such, Attune•ED takes a relational approach to emotion regulation by understanding the science behind how relationships affect emotional regulation. The way you interact with yourself and others sets the groundwork for a healthy self-concept and nervous system, and healthy relationships.

Key Concepts for Maintaining Mental & Emotional Health

As a trauma-informed curriculum, Attune•ED emphasizes three major concepts integral to helping us all stay within healthy stress levels: Choice, Attunement, and Co-regulation:

1) **Choice**

   Choice is an essential part of learning to regulate emotions for several reasons. For many who have experienced trauma, not having had the choice to take care of themselves is a lived reality. Providing yourself and others opportunities to choose what works and doesn't for mental health allows for a sense of agency and self-discovery. What works for you may not work for your partner or others. Often feeling you have no choice in a situation can increase stress. Again, you cannot change the fact that you may not have choices in some areas of your life, but working to increase freedom and choice in others can help decrease stress and increase wellbeing.

2) **Attunement**

   Attunement is the ability to know and understand your own emotions and those of others. This level of awareness is often called emotional intelligence. When you can name and understand what you are feeling, you are better able to act and communicate effectively. When you work to understand your emotions, you increase your emotional intelligence. Research has shown that being good at emotional intelligence increases physical wellbeing.[12]

3) Co-Regulation

Another facet of emotional intelligence, co-regulation refers to a two-way communication of emotions that results in overall less distress. Your nervous system is interwoven, and you have the ability to calm or excite a situation with the way you move, speak, and breathe. Sometimes, one person is in a position of greater responsibility to regulate the behavior of another, as with parents and children.

Attune·ED: Workbooks 1 & 2

Attune·ED is divided into two manuals: **Workbook 1** focuses on developing **self-awareness and self-regulation skills**, and **Workbook 2** focuses on **interpersonal awareness**, including compassion, empathy, and connection with others.

In this **Workbook 1**, we introduce core concepts of mental health and mindfulness skills that promote mental health. Each chapter is based on one of the five aspects of self-relating: Observer Self, Breath, Emotions, Thoughts, and Body. This structure provides a clear path toward grasping core concepts of mental health and mindfulness. It also clarifies the purpose and appropriateness of each mindfulness exercise.

Chapter 1 Mental Health & Mindfulness

This chapter defines what mental health is and how to cope with everyday stressors. It also defines mindfulness and how to use mindfulness practices to stay healthy.

Chapter 2 Relationship with the Observer Self

This chapter creates the foundation for mindful living by teaching how to observe thoughts, emotions, breath, and the body with curiosity and self-compassion. Doing so, in turn, helps focus attention on what is important rather than getting caught up in every thought or emotion.

Chapter 3 Relationship with Breath

This chapter covers observing and regulating the breath to instantly calm the body and mind. The breath is key to stress reduction and to the ability to manage difficult emotions skillfully. When there is a healthy relationship with the breath, it is a powerful ally.

Chapter 4 Relationship with Emotions

The ability to monitor, manage, and communicate emotions is key to self-awareness, emotional regulation, and social competence. This chapter teaches the physiological link between emotions, thoughts, and the body as well as skills that increase emotional awareness.

Chapter 5 Relationship with Thoughts

In this chapter, you learn how to observe your thoughts and gain greater perspective through mindfulness. Activities in this chapter encourage flexible thinking, which is a prerequisite to emotional regulation and problem solving.

Chapter 6 Relationship with the Body

This chapter builds upon the knowledge learned in the previous five lessons to highlight connections between the mind and body. It emphasizes developing a compassionate relationship with the body by using mindful body movement to regulate the nervous system; understand self-care needs such as hunger, fullness, rest, and relaxation; and focus attention. This kind of physiological regulation is key to stress reduction, self-management, and mental and emotional wellbeing and learning.

We know there are many ways to enhance mental health. There is no one way that works for everyone. We hope that our offerings in this book provide the framework to explore what works specifically for you, and help you cope with stressors in healthier ways; help you feel more agency in addressing problems; and that you feel well enough to experience life's joys, beauty, and moments of deep connection.

We also know that there are many sources of stress outside of your control, such as a challenging work environment, discrimination, financial difficulties, and climate change. Much of mental health work lies in changing the systems where we live and work. However, we hope the skills we teach help each of us gain more agency over our lives and become better advocates for the things we believe in.

> **As mental health therapists, we ourselves use the skills covered in this book, every day, to stay emotionally healthy, and it is with deep connection, gratitude, and humility that we take this journey with you.**

Chapter 1

Mental Health & Mindfulness

Mental health is health.

Key Mental Health Concepts

- Mental Health
- Window of Tolerance
- Mindfulness
- Metacognition
- Observer Self
- Neuroplasticity

What Is Mental Health?

The World Health Organization (WHO) defines **mental health** as a "state of wellbeing"; this means being able to have intense emotions or all kinds of thoughts while still following our values, living a meaningful life, and being able to contribute to society.[1] Life can be both wildly exciting and extremely difficult. When we are mentally and emotionally healthy, we can handle life's ups and downs. It is important to learn to be with intense emotions without being overwhelmed by them, and to know how to recover when we do feel overwhelmed. It is also important to know what gives our life meaning and makes us feel safe and motivated.

Window of Tolerance: A Key Concept for Mental Health

We begin with a key concept called the **Window of Tolerance**, a model of how our nervous system responds to stress that was developed by psychiatrist Daniel J. Siegel.[2] It is a fundamental tool for getting to know yourself better, what your emotional tendencies are, and how to help yourself when you feel distressed. Figure 1 shows the Window of Tolerance and two other zones.

When we are living or operating in the middle section, inside our emotional Window of Tolerance, our nervous system is pretty balanced. It is the state of mind where creativity, learning, playfulness, and relaxation can exist, and we feel like we can handle life's moment with grace—a car in front of us that seems to be driving purposefully slowly when we are late; our partner's clothes strewn all over the floor; a friend who has texted to cancel a date—for the third time.

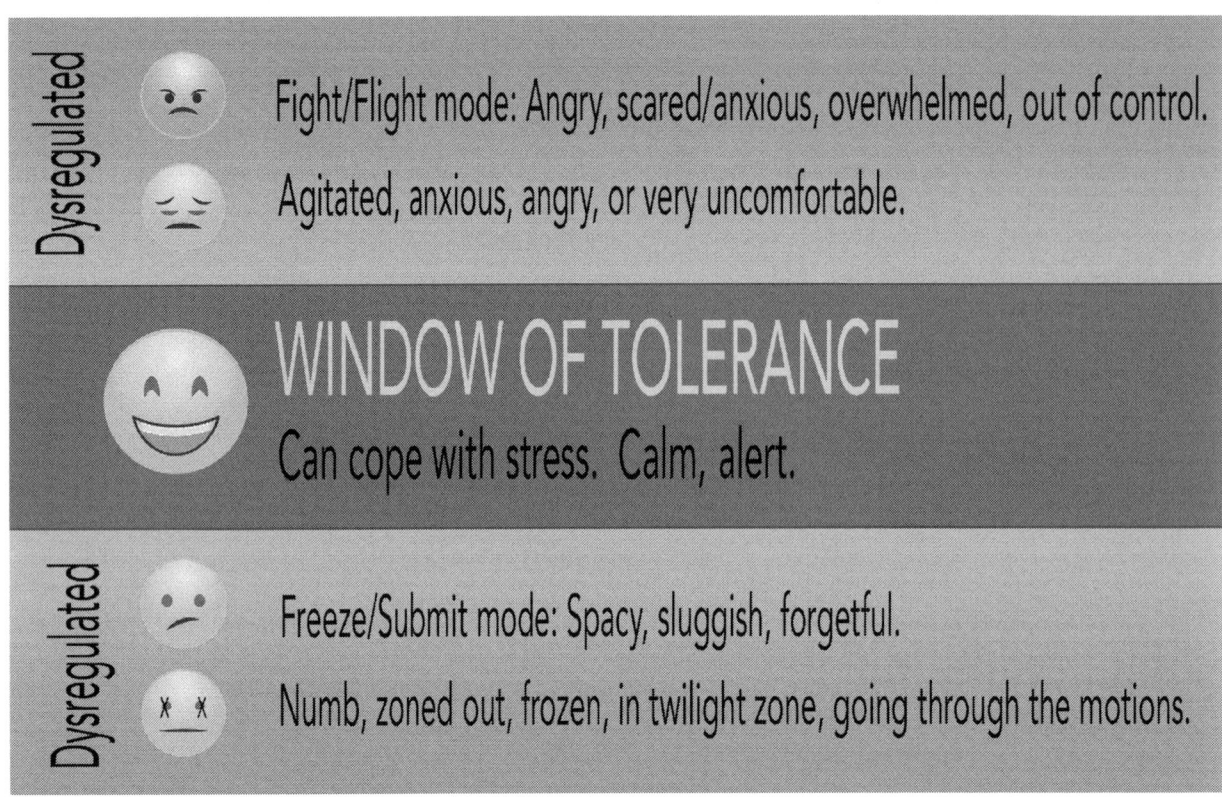

Figure 1. Window of Tolerance.

The Window of Tolerance can get wider or narrower.

One way that people describe having a narrow Window of Tolerance is by stating, "I am at the end of my rope!" Being able to identify and communicate the point of being "at the end of your rope" before losing control is the crux of emotional regulation. At this point, you are still in your Window of Tolerance, but it is narrowing.

Getting to know yourself and the very personal techniques that keep your Window wide helps you stay regulated and healthy. We are all different, with unique circumstances and physiology that affect our tolerance levels. Some people are born with highly sensitive nervous systems; some get more sensitive because of trauma; and others live life with a system that comes back into homeostasis with relative ease and stays open much of the time.

When we become overwhelmed by our emotions, we lose control because our ability to cope narrows, and we move outside of our emotional Window of Tolerance. At this level of stress, our nervous systems go into hyperarousal or hypoarousal mode, often described as "fight or flight" or "freeze or submit," respectively. These modes are shown in Figure 1 in the zones above and below the Window of Tolerance.

When we are outside our Window, we cannot think straight and are very reactive. This level of stress may happen when we are very hungry, tired, angry, or scared. This is an adaptive response to danger that developed to allow us to react without thinking in situations of extreme danger.

But in the modern world, we often go into fight, flight, freeze, or submit (FFFS) because of chronic stress or events that are not life-threatening. During these times, we honk incessantly at the car in front of us, snap at our partners, and text something we regret to a friend. The difference between these scenarios is not the events happening to us, but whether they shift us outside our Window of Tolerance once they occur.

Dr. Siegel uses the following example: When you take a spoonful of salt and mix it in a glass of water, the water will be very salty. But if you take that same spoonful of salt and mix it in a bathtub, you will hardly notice it. It is not the amount of salt or the problem that changes, it is the size of the container.[3] You can learn ways to widen your emotional Window so you can better handle life's ups and downs.

How to Use the Window of Tolerance?

Checking in with the intensity of your emotions can help you take care of yourself and know when you need to take a break or relax. There are daily practices or skills to help you live with more emotional tolerance so small things don't make you reactive, and you are able to access more gratitude and joy. Again, mental health is not about avoiding difficult events or emotions, but increasing your ability to handle them with skill.

The Window of Tolerance is the basis to explore these stressors that push you to the point of becoming overwhelmed. Mental and emotional health depends on the ability to move as quickly as possible from being outside the Window of Tolerance to back inside it, to a place of emotional balance.

We have identified three core qualities that help us stay inside the Window of Tolerance: centered, connected, and compassionate. They are not goals to achieve, but are more like values to keep moving toward. It's like when you want to head east and start driving in that direction. You never actually get to a place called "east," but going east guides the trajectory of your journey.

The Three Cs for Staying in Your Window

Centered: When we are centered, we can have intense emotions or thoughts without getting completely overwhelmed by them. We stay in an optimal zone of relaxation, and if we encounter a highly distressing event, we return to a healthy state as quickly as possible. We can practice being centered and can develop awareness of when we are and are not in this zone.

Connected: Being in a healthy relationship with both ourselves and others is central to our sense of wellbeing. A healthy relationship with oneself includes being able to be attuned to, but not enmeshed with, thoughts, emotions, breath, and the body. Similarly, healthy relationships with others means being treated respectfully and being able to attune to other people's thoughts and emotions.

Compassionate: Self-compassion helps us stay in our Window of Tolerance. When we treat ourselves and others with kindness and concern, we improve our health and sense of wellbeing. Self-compassion has been shown to improve mental and emotional health, empathy, and interpersonal relationships as well as academic achievement.[4] Being compassionate toward ourselves and others leads to increased calm and healthy connection.

What Is Mindfulness?

Sherry really wanted to hang out with her kids on her day off. Her plan was to get ingredients for a cake, bake together with them, and then have a family movie night. But taking a glance at the household mess, and she couldn't help herself—she started a quick clean-up. Then she noticed someone had called while she was working, and called them back. After she hung up, she opened an app on her phone and scrolled through social media—for an hour. Hours later, she realized she hadn't done anything she planned, and the day was almost over.

Carlos decided to surprise his wife for their anniversary. He went to buy her flowers and a necklace. While at the mall, he stopped by the electronics store to check out the newest big screen TVs. An hour later, he had checked out almost all the newest electronics, and he realized he was late for their anniversary dinner.

With so many demands on our time, including screens and messaging, it is very easy for our awareness and attention to be pulled away from what we value. **Mindfulness** helps us keep our lives aligned to our values. Mindfulness is defined as 1) increasing our awareness, and 2) paying attention to the present moment without immediate judgment. This may not seem particularly revelatory, but let's explore more the power of awareness and nonjudgmental attention to understand the significance of mindfulness in situations like the ones described above, and then more stressful, emotionally challenging ones.

The Power of Awareness

How amazing is it that, as humans, we can think back in time or imagine the future. We can be aware of whether our thoughts are racing or our minds are calm. We can describe how we are feeling.

That awareness about ourselves, how we are feeling physically and emotionally, is called self-awareness. Our level of self-awareness distinguishes us from other animals. It is an incredibly powerful ability that has the potential to greatly impact our mental and emotional health as well as the trajectory of our relationships and the world around us. It gives us the ability to respond skillfully rather than react impulsively. Humans are one of the few animals who can think about ourselves with such perspective, like being able to watch ourselves in a movie. Without the power of awareness, we would just react to our thoughts, emotions, and environment like many other animals: running from loud noises, chasing squirrels into dangerous traffic-filled roads, and scuttling to hide under a rock every time we heard footsteps five feet away. What these animals lack is the power of perspective.

This perspective gives us some space between ourselves and our thoughts, feelings, and sensations. When this skill is applied to observing our thought process, it's called **metacognition**. Metacognition is defined as the awareness and understanding of one's own thought process.

A saying that captures this concept is "regulate before you communicate." When we have self-awareness, we can choose to do something different than what we immediately think or feel. Like not sending a hurtful text message when we are really angry and waiting until we are calm before we text. Or like keeping track of the time while checking emails or hanging out in our favorite store. With mindfulness practices, we can increase our awareness of what is going on internally and pause before we react to our emotions.

> **Increasing our awareness allows us to respond thoughtfully rather than react impulsively so we can make healthier choices.**

Even though we as humans have this ability to be mindful, we often don't use it. Sometimes we do not regulate before communicating and say things we wished we hadn't; we do not engage what we call our **Observer Self**, and take a pause, and name and observe our thoughts and emotions without getting caught up in them. Instead, we get enmeshed with our emotions, which might cause us to lash out at a loved one; stay home sick because we have to give a presentation at work; or even just space out or go into autopilot and spend all day on Instagram without realizing it. (We do a complete exploration of the Observer Self in Chapter 2 Relationship with the Observer Self.)

Reacting mindlessly or without perspective makes life a lot harder and often keeps us from living our lives to the fullest. Reacting, rather than responding thoughtfully to events in life, also tends to increase stress and anxiety. Increasing our metacognition, our awareness and understanding of our thought process, allows us to respond thoughtfully so we can make healthier choices.

The Power of Attention

The second mindfulness power humans possess is the ability to focus our attention wherever we choose. Our attention can shift without us even knowing it. We can get lost in our thoughts or caught in an emotion. It takes effort and practice to train our minds to focus on what we choose. We will learn throughout the book the extent to which our attention affects our lives.

When you think about it, being in control of attention is one of the most powerful tools we can possess. Attention directs the flow of energy from our mind. If a cat suddenly ran across the room, or if someone slammed the door as they came in, what do you think you would do? Your attention would go directly to the cat or in the direction of the loud noise. Right? Attention changes your behavior in an instant. In those types of instances, we are not consciously controlling our attention; our attention is being grabbed by something in the environment.

This attention-grabbing can also happen inside our minds. For instance, we may be sitting at our desks, trying to pay attention to the work at hand, but a memory or thought keeps popping into our heads. We may begin to daydream about the memory, or maybe about an argument we had at home, or what we want to do after work. These thoughts grab attention in the same way as the cat or the notebook.

Mindfulness practices were developed to help with this. By consciously focusing your attention for a period of time, you increase your ability to control your attention. This then enhances the ability to focus attention on what is important and stay in the present moment. We liken it to training the brain as if we were training for a marathon. You begin with small runs, and then build endurance until you are running more miles than you ever thought you could. You would never have been able to do that unless you trained slowly and carefully, building strength and stamina.

This attitude of openness is often called having a "beginner's mind." It refers to the eagerness and lack of preconceptions when studying a subject like a beginner would (even when studying at an advanced level). When we stay open and curious rather than becoming reactive and judgmental, we can remain healthier and inside our Window of Tolerance.

Sometimes, when we are accustomed to reacting in our "usual" ways, these mental habits may seem too difficult to change. However, there is some exciting neuroscience that helps us understand that our mental patterns are flexible, and that practicing new skills can help make new pathways in the brain.

Anatomy & Physiology: Neuroplasticity—What We Practice Grows Stronger

When we practice something over and over again, like learning a new language or playing a musical instrument, we are changing our brain. This ability of the brain to change and grow (or shrink) over time is called **neuroplasticity**.

Our brains are made of about 100 billion cells called neurons. These neurons communicate with each other through connections called synapses. There are about 1 quadrillion synapses in our brains. That's 1,000,000,000,000,000 or 1,000 trillion synapses![5]

Each time our brain learns something new, like how to put together a table from Ikea, our neurons create a new synapse with each other. Existing connections can also grow stronger. And sometimes when we don't use something we know, we forget and lose a connection, or the connections grow weaker. Like after you learn a new language and don't use it for three years!

Neuroplasticity can also be compared to how social media works. If a tweet or a video gets a lot of attention and shares, it grows stronger. More and more people connect to it and see it. Maybe it even goes viral. But if it doesn't get much attention, then it dies out.

Our neurons are like viral tweets or posts, and the synapse connections are the likes and shares. The stronger our synapse connections, the stronger this part of our brain is. So when we learn a new dance or song, we are creating new synapses and strengthening related skills that are already there, like how to maintain balance, remember sequences, or memorize lines.

In fact, brain scan studies of professional athletes show that their areas of the brain related to controlling movement are bigger than that of other people. Neuroplasticity has shaped their brains in those areas. Brain scan studies have also shown that mindfulness increases the number of neurons and synapses in our prefrontal cortex.[6-8] This is the part of our brain responsible for making wise decisions not based on pure emotion, like when we decide not to yell at someone even though we feel very angry. Mindfulness practice also shrinks the amygdala, which is the part of the brain that takes over when we feel very scared.

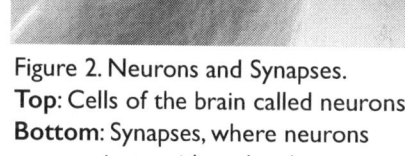

Figure 2. Neurons and Synapses.
Top: Cells of the brain called neurons.
Bottom: Synapses, where neurons communicate with each other.

When incorporating mindfulness into our lives, we actively shape the brain. Thanks to neuroplasticity, the areas of the brain related to memory, self-control, empathy, and compassion can, and do, grow bigger. Mindfulness also helps shrink areas of the brain like the amygdala that are related to "flipping our lids"—reactively losing our temper or becoming emotional.

Putting It Into Practice!

By learning about and practicing mindfulness, we are taking care of our mental and emotional health. Practicing mindfulness can actually change the structure of our brains to function more effectively, balance our nervous systems, and help us stay emotionally and physically healthy.

Through neuroplasticity, practicing mindfulness gives us more control over ourselves and our ability to be kind to others. We all know that what we practice grows stronger. So, turn to the next page, and let's go practice!

Fill in the Window of Tolerance Worksheet

*Using the blank worksheet on the next page,
answer the following questions.*

- Think for a moment about how you feel when you are inside your Window of Tolerance? How do you breathe? How would you describe your attention, your body sensations, and facial expressions? How would someone know looking at you that you are in your Window?

- What do you look or feel like when you get outside your Window? How would you describe your attention, your body sensations, and facial expressions? How would someone know looking at you that you are in your window?

- Do you tend to go into fight/flight or freeze/submit mode? How do they look different for you?

- Think of four things that typically get you out of your Window.

- Write four things that help you get back into your Window. Are they different if you are in fight/flight than freeze/submit?

- What are four activities that help your Window stay wide? These are things you do regularly to help you stay open and feel balanced emotionally. For example, going to the gym, having time to yourself, expressing things that are bugging you, connecting with friends, or being in nature.

For sample, filled-in Window of Tolerance Worksheets, turn to pages 18–20.

WINDOW OF TOLERANCE WORKSHEET

Overwhelm: Fight or Flight

Feels/Looks Like

_____

_____

_____

_____

What Helps

_____

_____

_____

_____

Window of Tolerance

Feels/Looks Like

_____

_____

_____

_____

What Helps

_____

_____

_____

_____

Overwhelm: Freeze or Submit

Feels/Looks Like

_____

_____

_____

_____

What Helps

_____

_____

_____

_____

EXPLORING YOUR WINDOW OF TOLERANCE
SAMPLE 1

Overwhelm: Fight or Flight

Feels/Looks Like

tight stomachache/nauseous

tingly/buzzing in body

temperature change — hot

short answers/snappy

finding something to fight about

What Helps

walking/heavy lifting

shaking it out

talking to a friend

singing

cold showers

Window of Tolerance

Feels/Looks Like

calm & energy

creative, smiling/body is still

open to new ideas/experiences

good listening/empathy

What Helps

being in nature

connecting w/ friends

sleep/good meals

engaging in meaningful experiences

time for self

Overwhelm: Freeze or Submit

Feels/Looks Like

people-please "yes yes"

low energy

procrastinating tasks

What Helps

funny videos

lying down

reducing responsibilities

gardening — sensory

petting dog

EXPLORING YOUR WINDOW OF TOLERANCE
SAMPLE 2

Overwhelm: Fight or Flight

Feels/Looks Like

Lack of effective communication

Lowered foresight

Sweating/queasy

Twitching

Decreased appetite

What Helps

Connecting to breath

Time alone/rest

Journal or meditation

Physical activity

Window of Tolerance

Feels/Looks Like

Empathy ≈ Awarenss of self-needs

Light and fluid

Effectively communicating

Able to make concise decisions

What Helps

Laughing

Communicating what I need

Nutrition

Overwhelm: Freeze or Submit

Feels/Looks Like

Morning moodiness

Seasonal depression

Can't make decisions or take action

↳ Analysis paralysis

Increased appetite

What Helps

Getting outdoors

Healthy sleep schedule

Connecting with love one ☆

Overwhelm: Fight or Flight

Feels/Looks Like

Tense

Red face

Racing thoughts

Perseverating on anger

What Helps

Getting away from a situation

Meditating

Journaling

Running

Window of Tolerance

Feels/Looks Like

Wide eyes

Curious

Smiling

Calm

What Helps

Regular exercise

Time to myself

Having fun

Strong relationships

Overwhelm: Freeze or Submit

Feels/Looks Like

CAn't think

Blank mind

No energy

Burnt out

What Helps

Walking in nature

Journaling

Strong boundaries

Yoga

Chapter 2

Relationship with the Observer Self

"Between stimulus and response lies a space. In that space lies our freedom and power to choose a response. In our response lies our growth and our happiness."

— Author Unknown

Key Mental Health Concepts

- Observer Self

- Metacognition

- Dialectical Behavioral Therapy (DBT)

- Acceptance and Commitment Therapy (ACT)

- Amygdala and the Prefrontal Cortex

- Fight, Flight, Freeze, Submit (FFFS)

- Anchoring Attention

Introducing the Observer Self

Think about the last time you drove or walked home and didn't notice or remember how you got there. Or how many times you have been in a meeting and completely "spaced out," with no idea what anyone was talking about. Or those times when you intended to look down at your phone for a second to check a text, and 20 minutes later, you were still looking at your phone. Those actions are like being on autopilot. Autopilot is when computers fly the plane without the direct control of the pilot. Many of us live a large part of our day on autopilot.

Now think instead about the alert you, who pops out of autopilot and suddenly realizes you arrived at work without even noticing how you got there. Or that conscious moment you come back from "spacing out" during a long conversation with a friend. It is like being transported from a faraway imaginary place back into the present moment. You come back into the moment with awareness. This awareness is the presence of what we call your **Observer Self**.

This chapter introduces the concept of the Observer Self, and how developing this part of yourself can help your mental and emotional health. This foundational concept is also referred to by many other names, such as the witness, wise mind, true self, and consciousness. We encourage you to use any version that resonates as true for you. The concept of the Observer Self is used in two of the main mindfulness-based psychotherapy approaches: dialectical behavioral therapy (DBT) and acceptance and commitment therapy (ACT, pronounced "act"). Both approaches (more completely described in the Supplemental Learning Section on the next page) have decades of research demonstrating strong support for their effectiveness with children and adults in managing anxiety and stress.

We can see from the above examples how mental health might be affected by living our lives on autopilot, or unconsciously, versus being mindful. When we are on autopilot, we are not the drivers of our lives, but are instead going along like robots, going through the motions. Practicing mindfulness means spending more time in conscious awareness, being present and attentive to what is going on, and spending less time on autopilot. This helps us live our values and be better partners and friends.

Self-awareness and emotional regulation are key indicators of mental and physical wellbeing. They are also precursor skills to interpersonal awareness and interpersonal skills. Observing thoughts and emotions—sometimes referred to as **metacognition**—and developing the ability to focus attention are foundational skills for self-awareness and emotional regulation. Being able to take a pause and observe thoughts and feelings without getting caught up in them is the ability to use your Observer Self.

People often say, "Take a break," or "Pause for a moment" when giving advice about dealing with stressful situations. However, if it were that easy, everyone would be peacefully pausing before communicating their frustration or anger. Instead, **pausing when emotional is one of the most difficult mental health skills to practice**. That's where developing a strong relationship with your Observer Self comes in. The Observer Self helps you identify where you are in relationship to your Window of Tolerance—whether you are comfortably in a place to cope with stress; are about to pop out of that place; or already have moved above or below it to a place of dysregulation (see Chapter 1 Mental Health & Mindfulness, Figure 1, to review the Window of Tolerance).

Understanding Your Observer Self

Knowing your Observer Self is key to living mindfully. It frequently helps you separate from your thoughts and emotions enough to respond rather than react. Take the example of a snow globe. When a person holds a snow globe in their hand, the water is clear, and the snow is settled on the bottom; they can see right through the globe to the other side, and the scene inside the globe is clear and visible. What happens when they shake the globe? Everything becomes cloudy, and they have no idea what is inside or on the other side.

When we get caught up in our thoughts or emotions without calm perspective, it is like that shaken snow globe—we get confused and can't think clearly. Emotions and thoughts can easily take over our full attention, leaving us believing we *are* our thoughts or our emotions! When we

DBT & ACT

Dialectical Behavioral Therapy (DBT)

Developed by psychologist Marsha Linehan, **dialectical behavioral therapy (DBT) is** a skills-based approach that focuses primarily on self-regulation.[1] "Dialectical" means to balance opposing forces, and in this case, refers to balancing intense emotion with a sense of calm. Most people already have some healthy coping strategies, like listening to music, a hobby, or talking with a friend. DBT helps identify these strategies and build upon them.

DBT is organized into four modules: Mindfulness, Emotional Regulation, Distress Tolerance, and Interpersonal Effectiveness. A core concept of the Mindfulness module is the "wise mind"—something everyone has (even if sometimes it doesn't feel like it!). The wise mind is used to observe thoughts and feelings nonjudgmentally in order to prevent being overwhelmed by them. In Attune•ED, the Observer Self is similar to the wise mind. We will continue to discuss aspects of the other three modules throughout the book.

Acceptance & Commitment Therapy (ACT)

Acceptance and commitment therapy (ACT, pronounced "act") was developed by psychologist Steven Hayes. ACT focuses on how we think about our thoughts and emotions by promoting a willingness to experience difficult emotions rather than avoid them in order to do things we want to do.[2] ACT helps people create meaningful lives that are true to their most precious values, including relationships, career, health, and spirituality, or just plain enjoying life. It starts with accepting where we are right now, and being willing to experience difficult emotions rather than trying to bury them. Mindfulness is an important tool in being able to observe emotions and thoughts with compassion. Through the practice of mindfulness, we become more compassionate observers of ourselves, expand our willingness to experience all emotions, and develop a lifestyle that moves us in the direction of our core values.

ACT also talks about a version of the Observer Self, what it calls "Self in Context." Self in Context means our ability to be aware and observe is like a container. Imagine a vase where flowers are put in, taken out, new ones put in, and so on. This is a metaphor for our relationship to thoughts and feelings, because while thoughts and feelings (the flowers) constantly come and go, our Observer Self (the vase) stays the same.

are viewing the world entirely through either lens—thoughts or emotions—we miss out on the big picture, and we get lost in the snowstorm. Operating purely on thoughts and emotions can cloud our deeper sense of self.

When we step back and become calm, we can gain perspective and reflect on what action to take. This helps us feel more in control of our lives and focus our energy on the things that are really important to us. Being able to observe the present moment without immediate judgment can help us stay clear and calm. When we are watching our own thoughts and feelings, we are able to have perspective and reflect on them. This skill is developed by staying present with the Observer Self.

We all have an Observer Self, and it allows you to focus your attention, change your behavior, and notice your thoughts and emotions. The Observer Self can be defined as the part of you that is always present and unchanging. It is always there for you, and you can tap into it anytime you want.

Anatomy & Physiology: The Observer Self

Two parts of the brain that affect our ability to access the Observer Self are the **amygdala** and the **prefrontal cortex** (see Figure 1).

The prefrontal cortex is the front part of the brain that computes, analyzes, makes decisions, and reasons. It can also *think about thinking*. This special ability makes humans very different from other animals.

But there is a catch—the prefrontal cortex can only do its job when the amygdala is not taking over.

The amygdala is an almond-shaped structure deep inside the brain. We have two amygdalae, one on each side of the brain. One of the main jobs of the amygdala is to alert us to danger, like a smoke detector alerts us to a fire in our house.

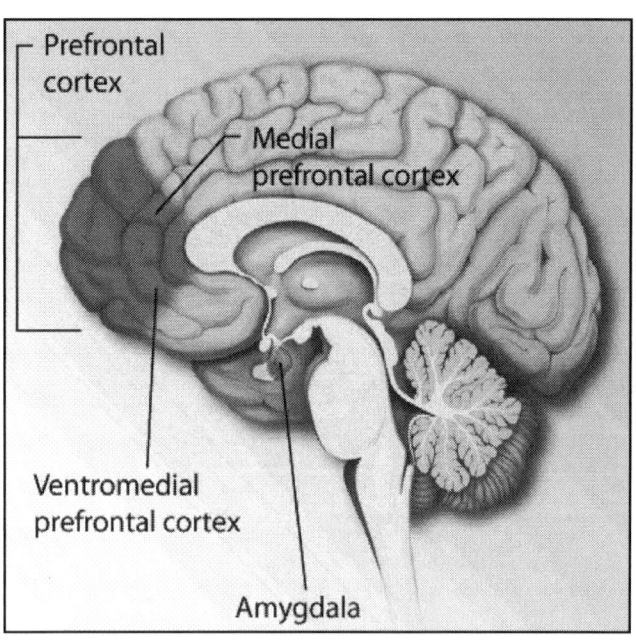

Figure 1. Prefrontal Cortex and Amygdala.
Image courtesy of the National Institutes of Health.

The amygdala is important for survival. In an emergency, the amygdala takes control of the brain and the prefrontal cortex shuts down.[3] For example, when we touch a hot stove, our amygdala kicks in to tell our body to move our hand—*now!* There is no time to think about whether or not we should move it. Usually, in life-threatening situations, people and animals go into something called **fight, flight, freeze, or submit (FFFS)** to survive. In the example, we retract our hand from a hot stove after touching it with the automatic reaction of flight. Sometimes, when we feel threatened, we fight or freeze.

> **The prefrontal cortex is the key to accessing your Observer Self.**

Sometimes, however, the amygdala sounds an alarm when there is no real danger. When this happens, it creates stress in the body even though it doesn't need to. It's like when the smoke detector goes off while we are just frying some food like bacon. If we smell smoke from upstairs, we may initially begin to panic, thinking there is a fire. What keeps us from panicking is our prefrontal cortex noting that it was just bacon and not a real fire.

Staying calm helps you keep your Observer Self online, and allows you to choose how to respond to a situation skillfully, rather than reacting without thinking, even when you feel anxious, angry, or hurt. You can distinguish real emergencies from times when you feel intensely but should probably not react.

Another way to understand this is to use your hand as a model of the brain, a technique developed by UCLA psychiatrist and mindfulness expert Daniel J. Siegel.[4] First, make a fist with your thumb tucked inside. The side with your fingernails showing represents your prefrontal cortex. The amygdala is the lower thumb joint (see Figure 3). When you are startled, sometimes the prefrontal cortex (the middle two fingers) flips up and leaves the amygdala in charge.

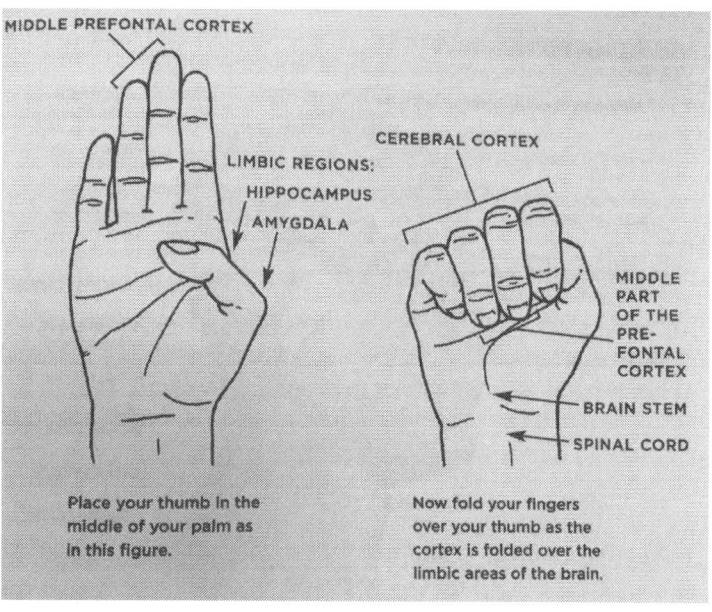

Figure 2. Dr. Daniel J. Siegel's "Hand Model of the Brain," as first described in *Siegel, D.J. (1999). The developing mind: Toward a neurobiology of interpersonal experience (1st ed.). New York, NY: Guilford Press.* © 1999 Mind Your Brain, Inc., and later depicted by visual image in *Siegel, D.J. (2010). Mindsight: The new science of personal transformation. New York, NY: Random House.* © 2010 Mind Your Brain, Inc.

According to research on human brains, mindfulness activities may develop the brain in helpful ways. If you practice using your Observer Self, you can keep your prefrontal cortex from shutting down when there is no real danger. As we saw in Chapter 1 Mental Health & Mindfulness, meditation is associated with increased thickness of the prefrontal cortex, the part of your brain that helps you to respond thoughtfully to situations. It is also linked to shrinking of the amygdala, the alarm system of the brain. By keeping communication flowing between the prefrontal cortex and the amygdala, you can think about whether or not there is an actual danger.

Developing a Relationship with Your Observer Self

There are many mindfulness practices that help develop your Observer Self. Some of the most common are Breath Awareness, Mindful Eating, and Anchoring with the Senses (the latter two practices appearing at the end of this chapter).

In each of these practices, the participant stays very present in the moment, without judgment and with full attention, increasing awareness of a chosen subject. We call this **anchoring attention**. This helps strengthen attention skills and pulls us away from operating on autopilot. The more these skills are practiced, the easier they are to use in everyday life.

These mindfulness exercises are common because they are relatively easy to access when you feel stressed or stuck in thoughts or emotions. Sometimes a thought or emotion becomes sticky, and you ruminate on it. Developing the ability to switch off of autopilot and move attention to something else can help gain perspective and reduce distress, which allows you to respond rather than react and problem-solve more effectively.

Again, noticing when you get stuck on an emotion or thought, and developing the ability to move toward and away from thoughts and emotions as desired, gives more control over choices and can reduce stress.

You can practice anchoring attention on any object, such as your breath, a leaf, or a flower, or the food you are eating. Beyond reducing stress, mindfulness allows you to appreciate beauty and experience happiness. The mind will wander back to sticky thoughts or emotions, and the practice is to gently bring the attention back to the anchor. Each time you catch yourself on autopilot, or lost in thoughts, and bring your attention back to the anchor, you strengthen your attention and awareness—your metacognition.

Anchoring Attention: The Check-In Wheel

To introduce the idea of relationship-building with your Observer Self, we will start with a check-in. The check-in is a brief scan that helps you get in touch with your Observer Self and helps you develop the ability to pause before reacting to thoughts and emotions. This practice is foundational and can be a brief daily or even more frequent mindfulness activity to help you become more aware and focus your attention. Regular check-ins help you notice how you are doing throughout the day and notice whether you are inside or outside your Window of Tolerance.

To help explain this practice, we use the concept of a wheel (see Figure 3), a modified version of Dr. Siegel's Wheel of Awareness.[5] In this model, the hub of the wheel represents the Observer Self, and the rim represents anything and everything you can observe in life.

For example, you can focus your attention on the outer world, on your inner experience, or on other people's thoughts and feelings. You can move your attention to the person sitting next to you, the daydream going on in your head, or the text coming onto your cell phone screen. These all would be part of the rim of the wheel.

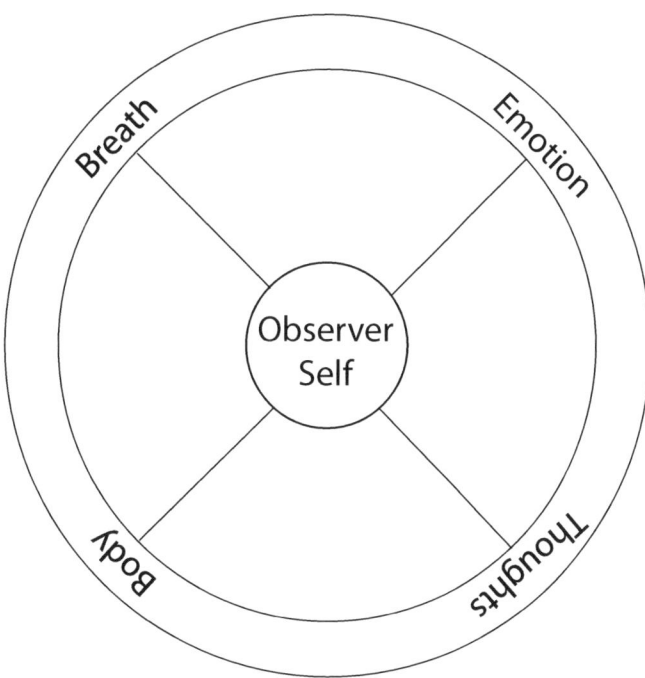

Figure 3. Check-In Wheel.

The constant is the Observer Self, which is the hub of the wheel. This is the part of us that can observe our thoughts and emotions without getting caught up in the round and round of the wheel. Knowing we can live in this place can help us stay calm and centered, instead of living on the rim, spinning and getting caught in thoughts and emotions.

> **For the check-in wheel practice, which begins on the next page, it's helpful to think of a flashlight shining on the places you want to focus your attention. During the check-in, you can observe, or shine, your attention onto your thoughts, onto emotions, or aspects of the body.**

NOTE: Link to audio at www.Attune-ED.com for a guided practice.

Practice 1: Using the Check-In Wheel

To get in touch with your Observer Self, you will practice checking in with your breath, body, thoughts, and emotions, as an observer. This will help you become more aware and focus your attention without getting caught up.

- To begin, take a moment to notice your breath.
- Is your breathing fast or slow? Does your breath go all the way into your belly, or is it shallow, stopping in your chest? You may notice the cool air coming in through your nose and the warm air flowing out.
- Any way you are breathing is just fine. We are simply here to observe and pay attention.
- Now shift your attention to your thoughts. What is going on up there? Are they calm or are there lots of thoughts? Are you worrying about something in particular today?
- Notice what you are thinking about, observing the thoughts as they come and go.
- Now move your attention to your emotions. You might notice that emotions are generally experienced in your body. Where are you experiencing emotions?
- Are they in your stomach? Your chest? Your throat?
- Do you feel a tightness or a feeling of warmth?
- Can you label what you are feeling? Happy? Sad? Anxious?
- Gently observe what is going on inside.
- Finally, check in with your body. To know how our bodies are, we usually need to move. In your seat or standing up, begin to move and stretch. Notice places where you might have some tightness or discomfort. Notice areas where you feel flexible or good.

REFLECTING ON THE PRACTICE

Take a moment:
- What did you notice that you were not aware of before the check-in?
- How might this help you today?

CHAPTER 2: LET'S PRACTICE (MORE)

Here are two additional practices that can help strengthen the ability to access your Observer Self: Practice 2: Anchoring with the Senses and Practice 3: Mindful Eating, on the next page. Either of these practices, or even taking a mindful walk where you intentionally focus on your surrounding and not on your thoughts, can help to reset and get you back into your Window of Tolerance.

Practice 2: Anchoring with the Senses

- Take a moment to get comfortable. Concentrate on your breathing.

- Gently draw your attention to 3 things you see in the room that you hadn't noticed before.

- Next, draw your attention to 3 sounds in the room, noting each one silently.

- Now, focus your attention to 3 things you feel through touch; this could be the sensation of your shirt on your skin, or your eyelids warming your eyes as you blink.

- Slowly release your attention from the senses and come back to focus on your breath.

REFLECTING ON THE PRACTICE

Take a moment:

- How did this activity make you feel?

- What was happening in your mind and body?

- Did it make you more anxious, or stressed, or less so?

- Did you notice things you hadn't noticed before?

Practice 3: Mindful Eating

The following script was written for use with an orange or tangerine but can be adapted for use with other types of food.

- Take a moment to get comfortable.

- Bring your attention to the fruit in front of you.

- Without touching it, observe the outside.

- Notice everything you can about how it looks on the outside.

- Take a moment to think about how this fruit got here, possibly beginning with when it was a seed all the way to the table in front of you.

- Now pick up your fruit and observe how it smells and feels, noticing its texture and temperature.

- Next, you can begin to peel it.

- Using your Observer Self, bring your attention to the peel, and try to notice all aspects of the peel.

- Then, you can begin to break it into segments or sections.

- Notice the pieces as whole units, and then break one in half.

- Take a moment to look into the piece and notice the insides.

- Now take a bite, chewing slowly and deliberately, noticing the taste and texture of the fruit in your mouth.

- As you swallow, try to follow the piece as far down your digestive track as possible, noting when you can no longer feel it.

REFLECTING ON THE PRACTICE

Take a moment:

- How did this activity make you feel?

- What was happening in your mind and body?

- Did it make you more anxious or stressed or less so?

- Did you notice things you hadn't noticed before?

Bonus Activity: Focus on What's Important

If you have time this week, try this activity to explore how you want to focus your attention.

- On a sheet of paper, draw two circles.

- Under or beside the first, list the things you spend your time and mental energy on. For example, you might spend most of your day thinking about work, cleaning the house, or worrying about money.

- Draw slices in the circle that represent about how much time you spend on each activity (mental or physical).

- On the second circle, draw the ways you want to spend your mental and physical energy. This chart represents your values and shows where you would like to focus your attention.

It is important to be kind and compassionate about your circles! It does not help to berate yourself for not living your values.

Instead, we are working toward being more conscious of our attention and actions, and will gradually, through frequent practice, work toward having these two circles become one. As you do, you may notice you feel better and have more energy.

Wrap-Up

Let's return to the idea of a trip home and social media binging for a minute.

Think about the last time you really looked around on a daily trip back to your house. Or those moments in life with a friend when you laughed until you cried. These are moments of being present and not on autopilot. Usually, these are the moments when we find meaning and joy in our lives.

Developing healthy relationships with your thoughts, emotions, and body begins with accessing your Observer Self. Your ability to use your attention well and increase your level of awareness (your metacognition) can help your physical and mental health, and decrease stress. The ability to observe your thoughts and emotions without getting caught up in them is a key skill in emotional regulation.

Chapter 3

Relationship with Breath

When we breathe shallowly or hold our breath, we are communicating to our body that we are in distress. Using breath wisely helps our body and mind.

Key Mental Health Concepts

- Autonomic Nervous System

- Distress Tolerance

- Sympathetic System and Parasympathetic System

We have all heard the advice, "Calm down and breathe," or "Take a deep breath." So, we all know that breath is somehow linked to calming down. Try being calm while you hold your breath. Not so easy, right? Now think about how you can stay calm by breathing slowly and deeply, even when scared. Breath has a lot of control over our nervous system and, therefore, our mental and emotional wellbeing. How exactly does this work? And how can you use breath to increase your mental health?

Most of the time, we breathe without thinking about it, in the same way that our hearts beat without our trying. The beauty of breath is that, unlike our heart rate, it is in our control. By intentionally changing the depth, duration, and frequency of breath, we can influence the **autonomic nervous system**, which regulates heart rate, the circulatory system, and the digestive system. Thus, through the breath, we can affect all these systems and the activities of the mind.[1,2]

Once you become more conscious of this relationship, **you can use breath as a powerful means to counter daily stress**. You can stay calmer during stressful events by slowing and deepening your breaths, or you can activate your nervous system by taking short, quick breaths. Humans are one of the only animals who can consciously control their breath to regulate their nervous systems. By modifying our breathing, we can change how we feel.

In this chapter, we will introduce to you the research behind the power of the breath in stress reduction, and will focus on how you develop a relationship with breath to help your body and mind feel better. Lastly, we provide breath-based practices that immediately calm the nervous system.

Anatomy & Physiology: How Does Breath Affect Your Nervous System?

The nervous system has two main parts: the part that you control on purpose, like moving your head, and the part that works without your thinking about it, like your heart beating. This second part is called the autonomic nervous system (ANS), which is divided into the **sympathetic system** and the **parasympathetic system**, pictured in Figure 1.

The sympathetic system is like the gas pedal in a car, while the parasympathetic sympathetic is like the brake. In times of crisis, the sympathetic system can rev you up, allowing you to react quickly—your heart races, your pupils dilate, and glucose floods your system.

The parasympathetic nervous system controls the body's ability to relax and counters the

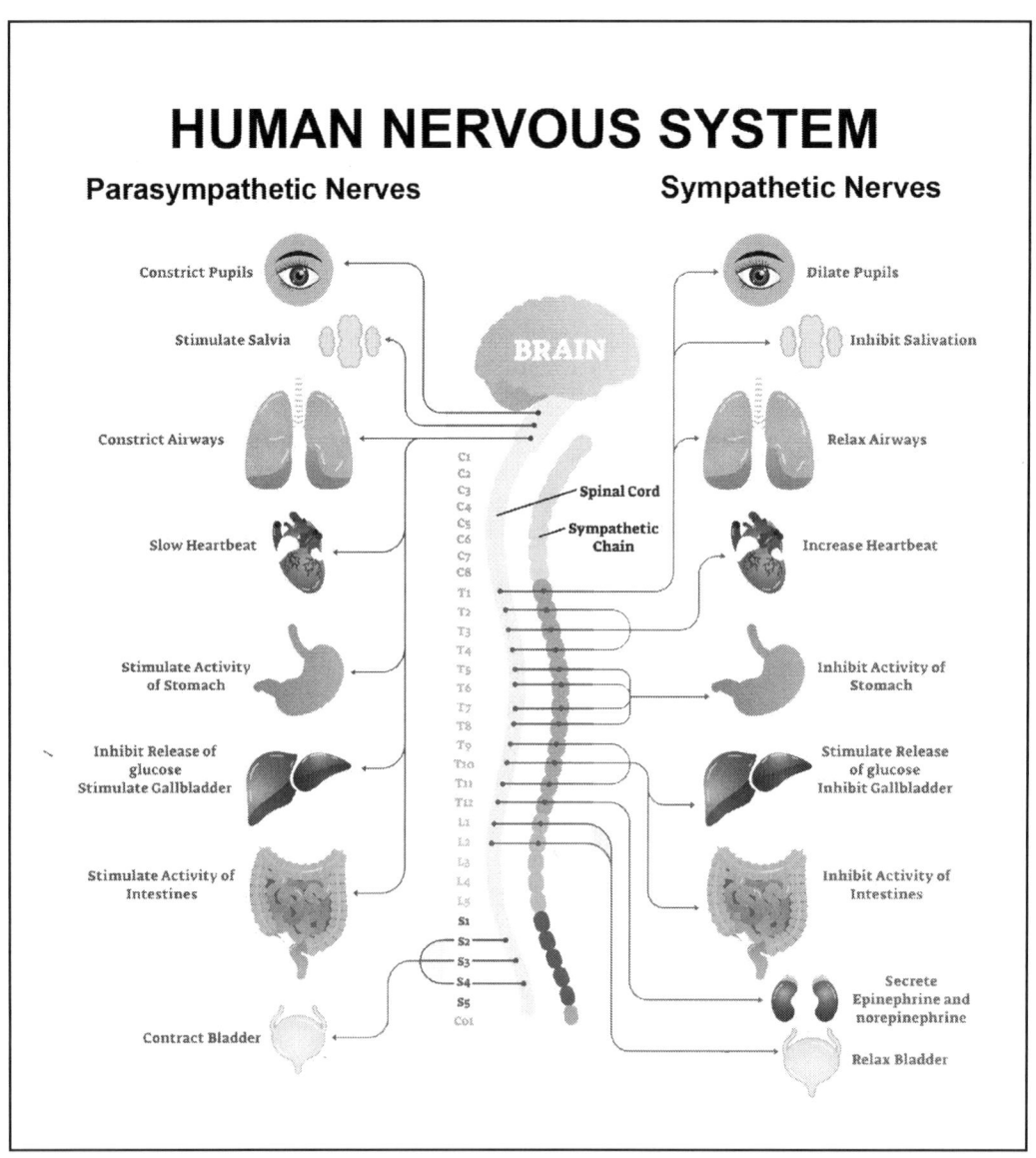

Figure 1. Human Nervous System: Parasympathetic Nerves and Sympathetic Nerves.

activation of the body by the sympathetic nervous system. When a danger has passed, your parasympathetic nervous system applies the brakes to help you regain calm, slowing the heart rate and returning body function to normal.

You can see that in order to operate in balance, you need control over both pedals. And you can develop this control through the breath. The beauty of breath is that, unlike your heart rate, it is directly in your control.

On the inhale, your sympathetic nervous system is engaged, and when you exhale, you engage your parasympathetic system. Breathing quickly can press on the gas pedal, inducing anxiety, while breathing deeply and extending your exhale can calm the body by initiating the parasympathetic nervous system, pressing on the brake pedal.

By intentionally changing the depth, duration, and frequency of breath, you can influence the autonomic nervous system. In other words, you can use the breath to directly affect your heartbeat, circulatory system, digestive system, and activities of the mind.[1,2] Breath can keep your nervous system in balance, and can keep the thinking part of your brain, the prefrontal cortex, online.

How Do You Use Breath to Affect Mood & Health?

Practicing breathing mindfully can help sharpen attention, balance the nervous system, and quiet the mind in situations where you might be reactive or where you would be better off staying calm.

You can use breath to do three things:[3]

1) **Anchor your attention to help you connect with the Observer Self.** [4,5]

   By simply becoming aware of the breath, you use the Observer Self to anchor attention to the present moment. This helps get you unstuck from distressing thoughts or emotions.

2) **Calm your nervous system.** [6–9]

   You can use breath as a mechanism to regulate the nervous system to bring it into the Window of Tolerance. For example, taking slower breaths and exhaling fully can help you feel less anxious because it helps activate the parasympathetic system. By doing this, you are using your breath as a mechanism to help regulate your nervous system and experience calmness within the body.

3) **Regulate your emotions.** [10,11]

   Intentionally changing how you breathe is another tool for regulating your emotions and staying within your Window of Tolerance. When you have more control over your attention and feel calmer, you have space to check in with yourself. You can use the Observer Self we talked about in Chapter 2 to notice what you are feeling and where you are in the Window of Tolerance. The breath becomes a guide that you can trust to help you.

Distress Tolerance

Distress tolerance is a term from dialectical behavior therapy (DBT) that simply means the ability to handle intense emotions.[12] It is an ability that grows stronger with practice. DBT (for a review, see p. 25) teaches distress tolerance skills that are specific coping strategies that help us get through tough situations. Sometimes, we do not have any control over a situation, like when we get laid off from a job, lose a loved one, experience racism or xenophobia, or have a stressful day in general. But mindfulness skills help us function as best we can under the circumstances.

It is important to recognize that distress tolerance is not about suppressing feelings or thoughts, but being able to cope with feeling in healthy ways. This results in the ability to experience them with less anxiety while maintaining our center. Distress tolerance skills offer the possibility that we don't have to be constantly blown away like a leaf in the wind by whatever is happening; instead, they offer the hope of self-control.

Using Breath as an Anchor for Our Attention

Much of mindfulness is related to gaining control over your attention so you can live life according to your own values rather than conditioned responses. The use of an anchor is a key mindfulness tool for focusing the mind. As discussed in Chapter 1 Mental Health & Mindfulness, our minds like to follow the shiniest object or the most intense headline. Some people call this "monkey mind." For us to get out of monkey mind and have more control over our attention, we need to develop the ability to focus.

For some people, the breath is a helpful anchor for their practice, as it is always with them and can be calming. However, for others, focusing on the breath can cause anxiety, and a better anchor might come from such things as noticing the cool air on your hands; feeling the pressure of your feet on the ground; or noticing the details of the leaves around you while walking your dog.

When we spend a few minutes each day focusing on our breathing, or any anchor, we train the brain to be one-pointed. This means we get out of monkey mind for a few minutes and consciously focus our attention.

Now, it doesn't really matter what you focus your attention on, and the idea of meditating on your breath, or a leaf, or the cool air on your skin may seem boring. And it can be! But once you begin to reap the benefits of the brain changes, you may see that the practice is a means to a calmer and more focused mind, which feels so much better than a frazzled monkey mind.

Many people ask the question, "Isn't mindfulness the same as flow or the experience I have when I play soccer or football, or watch TV? All my attention is going to one place, and I am no longer in monkey mind."

Flow and focused attention in any manner can be beneficial to our health, as they allow for breaks from worry and conditioned thinking. However, mindfulness involves consciously focusing your attention. Being caught up in a football game on TV is a great distraction from the stress of daily life, but a bit different than training your attention to purposefully focus on what is happening in the moment or focusing purposefully on an anchor to settle the mind and disentangle it from sticky thoughts and emotions.

Now let's practice!

CHAPTER 3: LET'S PRACTICE

Practice 1: Anchoring with the Breath

In this activity, the Observer Self is used to focus the breath, and the breath acts as an anchor for attention. You may notice that when you focus on your breath, you don't think about as many other things. This is how we anchor our attention, which can help decrease rumination and related stress. Breath is always with us, so it is an easily accessible tool whenever we need to gently pull our attention away from distressing thoughts and back into the moment.

Doing this may also change your physiology immediately, bringing you back into a somewhat calmer state. In addition, people are healthier when they feel more control in their lives. We can use our Observer Self to guide our attention and have a better relationship with our minds, allowing us to spend more time focused on what gives our life meaning.

(PRACTICE 1 continued on next page)

(PRACTICE 1 continued from previous page)

Important Note: Research has found that for some people focusing on the breath increases anxiety. If you experience anxiety while doing any of these exercises, it is okay to shift attention to something pleasant. For example, a favorite place or something you are looking forward to. Or find focus by taking a walk around the block, really observing your neighborhood like you are seeing it for the first time. These are all possibilities you can explore other than focusing on breath. We learn from what works, and we also learn from what doesn't work for us. Please feel free to try practices and notice your preferences.

- Begin by getting settled in your chair. Spend a minute noticing any tension in the body . . . shoulders, jaw, belly . . . and see if you can gently release any tension.

- Now bring your attention to your breath. You may close your eyes if it feels comfortable, or keep them open and softly gaze at the floor.

- Bring your attention to the inhale and the exhale. Watching the rhythm of the breath.

- Your shoulders may rise and fall.

- You may notice the cool air coming in through the nose and the warm air releasing. You don't need to change your breathing, just watching it as it is, in whatever way you are breathing, is fine.

- Take another minute to focus on your breathing. If your mind wanders, just gently bring it back to the breath as an anchor. Each time you notice the mind wandering, you are doing the practice.

- Now slowly shift your attention back to the room. You can open your eyes if they were closed and focus your gaze on the area around you. You might stretch your neck, arms, or legs.

REFLECTING ON THE PRACTICE

Take a moment:

- What did you notice about this experience?

- Did you get calmer or more anxious?

- What happened in your mind?

- How does your body feel?

Practice 2: Extended Exhale to Come Back into Balance

This second activity helps you explore how much more control over your nervous system you have than you probably think. The activity highlights the ability to control breathing by accessing the parasympathetic nervous system (the brake pedal). As you realize you can change your breathing and heart rate throughout the day, you also learn that you can excite or calm the nervous system to help with mood and health.

- Take a moment to get comfortable.

- Again, feel free to close your eyes or keep them slightly open.

- Begin by bringing your attention to your breath; watching the inhale and exhale, the ebb and flow of the breath.

- Watch three cycles of breathing, in and out, holding your attention on the breath.

- On the next inhale, count slowly, noticing the count that leads you to a comfortable stopping point where you are full of breath without any distress.

- Then exhale, finding a comfortable stopping place where most of the air has been released.

- Now count in and out the same number of times, creating more equal breathing; slowly count the same number on your inhale and exhale; do this for 3 breath cycles.

- Finally, do the same counting in and out of your breathing, but extend your exhale two counts: inhaling your original number of breaths . . . and then exhaling two counts longer.

- Now gently shift your attention back into the room, noticing the things around you. Feel free to roll your neck, wiggle your fingers, and arch your back in your chair.

REFLECTING ON THE PRACTICE

Take a moment:

- How does your body feel?

- What changes did you notice, if any, in your mind?

Wrap-Up

Developing a conscious relationship with your breath can help you emotionally and physically by acting as an anchor for your attention, to calm your thoughts and by activating the brakes of your nervous system. It is always with you, so you can always use breath as a tool for getting centered. The more you practice regularly, the better you will be at using it when stressed, allowing for a little space to respond rather than react. The next time you are under stress at home or work, try to pause and do the Anchoring the Breath practice on p. 39, or the Extended Exhale practice on the previous page.

Chapter 4

Relationship with Emotions

Emotions are always changing. They may feel stuck, but if you watch very closely, they are more like waves on the ocean.

Key Mental Health Concepts

- Emotional Intelligence

- Top-Down and Bottom-Up Processing

- Acceptance and Commitment Therapy

- Name It to Tame It

- Emotional Granularity

- Level of Emotion vs. Level of Problem

- Vagus Nerve

Emotions can be both our best and worst guides. Sometimes we become enmeshed with our emotions and cannot see clearly—the level of our emotions doesn't match the level of the problem. Learning to regulate our emotions is fundamental to a healthy life. By developing a healthy relationship with emotions and learning to use our Observer Self, we can help gain perspective, stay in our Window of Tolerance, and develop **emotional intelligence**.

In this chapter, you will learn essential skills for emotional regulation. These include identifying and labeling emotions, evaluating their intensity, and increasing tolerance of uncomfortable emotions.

What Are Emotions?

Emotions can be defined as sensations and physical responses to internal or external events that we make meaning out of.[1] For example, we may feel butterflies in our stomach as the emotion underlying excitement.

Emotions can let us know something is wrong or can guide us toward passion and meaning in life. However, if we are enmeshed or stuck in them, we become confused, stressed, and reactive.

To understand emotions, you must use both your mind and your body. When is the last time you felt your heart race, you had butterflies in your stomach, you blushed, your hair stood on end, or you felt as if you were punched in the stomach when you got rejected? These are examples of how emotions are experienced in the body.

You have receptors in the brain that send signals down to the body that make you physically feel emotions. Likewise, you have receptors in your body that send information up to your brain that help you feel emotions. We call the first process **top down**, and the second, **bottom up**. (See the Anatomy & Physiology section of this chapter, on p. 52, for a more in-depth explanation.)

If you feel anxious just thinking about a snake, or something else that scares you, that is an example of a **top-down process**. On the other hand, if you suddenly see a snake slither away from your path, you might automatically feel fear in your body, even before thinking. This is an example of a **bottom-up process**.

Similarly, you can sink into a hot bath and feel relaxation take over your nervous system, or you can just think about sinking into a hot bath and experience some of the same feelings. Scenarios like these demonstrate how your emotions are constantly changing and responding to your thoughts and experiences. The body and brain will have similar reactions, whether it is bottom-up information from your body or top-down information from your thoughts.

You Are Not Your Emotions

Tyron really wanted a new job. He had received excellent reviews as a social studies teacher over the last five years. There was an administrative position at the central office that fit his interests perfectly. He had submitted his resume and been offered an interview. As part of the interview, he would have to give a 20-minute presentation. As the day got closer, Tyron began to question his ability to get through the interview. He imagined freezing and losing all words. Two weeks before the interview, he started to have difficulty sleeping and to get stomach aches. He was also agitated and found himself snapping at his family. He began to think about cancelling the interview.

This is the power of emotions. Here again, you can see the interrelationship between emotions, thoughts, and the body. Tyron's fear was showing up in his body, and was so intense, he was considering giving up on his dream. Emotions can inhibit us from doing what we want. Recognizing that you are more than your emotions is a key to good mental health. Like in the Check-In Wheel exercise in Chapter 1 Mental Health & Mindfulness, you can use your Observer Self to examine your emotions and remind yourself you don't need to be ruled by them.

In mindfulness practices, we focus on several statements to create some distance from our emotions and help observe them without being consumed by them.

- You are not your anxiety, your anger, or your excitement. You *have* anxiety, anger, or excitement, which is reflected in these "I" statements: "I feel angry versus I am angry," or "I am anxious versus I have anxiety."

- You can listen to your emotions and they can guide you, or you can decide not to listen to them.

- It is normal and adaptive for intense events to affect your body's ability to emotionally regulate, and there are skills you can learn to help heal.

- There are times in your life, around age three, adolescence, and mid-life, when you often have more intense emotions because of what is happening in your brain and body.

- Everybody is different, and some people feel emotions more or less intensely than others. We all have different Windows of Tolerance.

Understanding emotions is related to overall health and wellbeing. It takes time and practice to get a better understanding of your unique emotional responses and how to use them wisely, to be able to answer questions like why did I react that way? What is making me so agitated? How do I communicate this effectively? Do I need to do anything to resolve these feelings?

Emotional Intelligence as a Tool for Emotional Regulation

Although **emotional intelligence** can have many meanings, one of the ways to view it is as a set of skills that can be learned.[2] There are at least three categories of these skills:

1) The ability to be aware of emotions and name them, otherwise known as emotional granularity.

2) The ability to use emotions for problem solving.

3) The ability to regulate emotions and help others regulate theirs.

The next section on acceptance and commitment therapy (ACT) and emotional granularity illustrates how these skills can be used to overcome anxiety.

Name It to Tame It & Emotional Granularity

Acceptance and commitment therapy (ACT) is a mindfulness-based approach to mental health.[3] One of its core principles is to develop a relationship with emotions, which increases our willingness to have and experience them while recognizing that we are bigger than our emotions. We see ourselves like a container for them, like a jar holding marbles. Remembering we are the jar helps keep us from losing our marbles! This is the *Acceptance* step. (See the brief introduction to ACT in the Supplemental Learning section of Chapter 2 Relationship with Emotions, p. 25).

The next step is *Commitment*—following through with doing something we care about even while experiencing intense emotions. In ACT, we learn to be more comfortable with our fears so they don't stop us from doing things. It doesn't mean the fears go away.

Using an ACT approach with Tyron and his anxiety about the interview, we would help him develop more awareness of his emotions, the first component of emotional intelligence. UCLA psychiatrist and mindfulness expert Daniel J. Siegel often uses the phrase "Name It to Tame It" to describe the regulating effect on the nervous system that merely identifying a feeling can have.[4] Instead of trying to avoid the interview and his feelings of anxiety, Tyron could explore his feelings more deeply.

Being able to feel and label emotions with precision is a skill called "emotional granularity." Research has found that practicing emotional granularity helps calm the nervous system and reduces the intensity of the emotions.[2]

In one study, researchers recruited participants who had arachnophobia, a phobia of spiders, and told them to walk toward a tarantula, although they could stop at any time.[5] Each participant was then instructed to do one of four things:

- Label their anxiety;

- Think differently about the spider so it seemed less frightening;

- Distract themselves from the anxiety; or

- Do nothing.

The researchers invited the participants to return to the lab and walk toward the tarantula again. The researchers measured how much the participants' palms were sweating, an indication of anxiety, and how close they were able to get to the tarantula. Those who had been instructed to label their emotions had the least physiological response and were able to get closest. In addition, the more emotions they could name, the less reactive they were and the closer they got to the tarantula.

In other research, practicing emotional granularity reduced the likelihood of acting aggressively.[2] There are also long-term benefits for physical health. People with higher emotional granularity see the doctor less often and need less medication. They also are hospitalized for shorter periods of time than others with the same illness.[2]

In Tyron's case, helping him recognize that he felt terrified and dreaded the interview instead of just identifying as "stressed" allowed him to better practice problem solving, the second component of emotional intelligence. Knowing he feels dread can help him question why he feels that way. He may realize he is worried he'll fail and make a fool of himself. After identifying this problem, he can respond rather than react to his intense feelings by developing strategies to help himself deal with the fear of failure. For example, he could garner support from friends and practice the interview and presentation a few times.

We know that practicing something we are afraid of doing helps us feel more confident. Tyron could also practice deep breathing and journal about why he wants to do the interview so his mind doesn't get hijacked by fear-based thoughts. With this plan, he will be able to practice the third component of emotional intelligence: managing his fear so that he can move forward with his goal of interviewing for the new job. In this way, Tyron is acting according to his values and not the level of his emotions.

Tools for Managing Emotions

How often do we let our emotions rule our decisions? Have you ever avoided a situation because you were afraid even knowing, as Franklin D. Roosevelt said, "There is nothing to fear but fear itself"? Emotions are powerful and can get in the way of living a meaningful and healthy life if left unchecked. Understanding emotions and our relationship with them can help us make healthier choices and allow us to follow our dreams rather than our fears.

The following sections review two ways you can view your Observer Self to help you understand your relationship with emotions to react more wisely in a situation.

Observer Self: Level of Emotion vs. Level of Problem

Emotions can feel big, but be about something small. For example, you may stay up all night worrying about a conversation you need to have with your partner. In the middle of the night, you may actually feel the problem is a 5 out of 5, with 5 being the highest severity—it can feel like if you don't say exactly the right thing the right way, the whole situation will blow up. Your body reacts as if it is encountering a life-or-death situation. This is an example of your thoughts telling your body you are in danger, or top-down processing. You are lying in bed, totally safe and sound, but are experiencing high levels of stress, imagining a worse-case scenario.

However, often what you are worried about isn't life-threatening. Even if there is a big conflict in your relationship, you can probably come up with a strategy to help resolve it, and it may actually improve your relationship or the situation. Other examples include:

- Being frozen with fear over public speaking.

- Getting furious that your partner keeps flipping the channels.

- Feeling embarrassed about a comment you made at a staff meeting.

- Feeling devastated by throwing an airball during a basketball game.

In all these cases, the problem is not as big as the feeling, and is something that you won't remember in a few days. Using your Observer Self, you can identify when you are having these kinds of feelings, to examine the level of the problem; you can increase awareness of the relationship between thoughts, emotions, and the level of a problem to work things out.

Differentiating the Levels

The scale in Figure 1 can help you learn to differentiate between the levels. You can fill in the circles to identify the intensity of the emotions and the level of a problem. The scale for Level of Problem can be explained as follows:

(1) **Momentary Problem**—You won't remember it tomorrow: The house is a mess; no one will go to the movies with you.

(2) **Little Problem**—You might remember it a week from now: The dishwasher breaks; you and your partner argue over whose family to visit over the holidays.

(3) **Medium Problem**—An event that could affect you for weeks to months: You're having a major operation; you've lost a best friend.

(4) **Big Problem**—An event that could affect you for many months or years: You were in an accident; lost a job; have been emotionally abused.

(5) **Emergency**—There is an immediate danger to self or others: You may need to call 911.

Note: Some issues like racism and other forms of discrimination may fall into more than one category. For example, a racial microaggression experienced at work may seem momentary but also feel like a big problem related to society as a whole.

Level of Emotion vs. Level of Problem

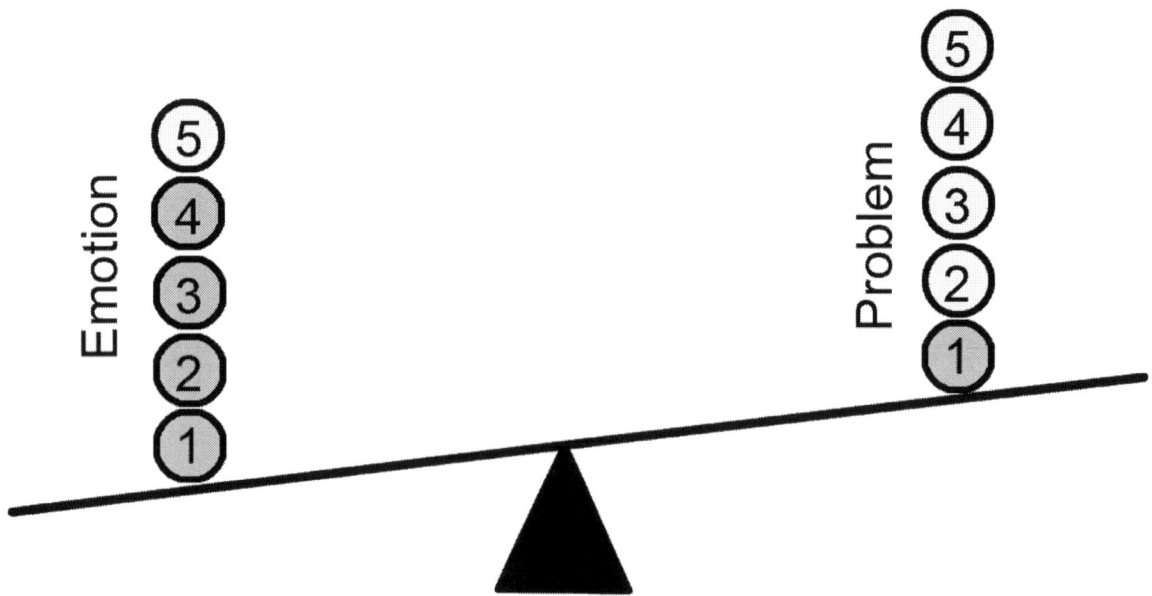

Figure 1. Level of Emotion vs. Level of Problem. Using this scale, you can fill in circles to identify the intensity of your emotions and the level of a problem. Here we show the emotion may be rated as a 4, but the problem in the end is rated as only a 1.

Separating thoughts from emotions and noticing the level of the emotion versus the problem can be extremely helpful when your fears are not at the level you imagine. You may just be thinking about something, but not actually experiencing it—and not be consciously aware of this distinction.

When you are more aware, for example, that emotions can be a 5 but that the *problem* may be a 2 or 3, you can better calm yourself and respond to the situation. Doing this can help you increase your emotional capacity to deal with difficulties in life. Rather than reacting to every emotion, you have the perspective to respond.

Observer Self: Emotions Come & Go

What do emotions have to do with mindfulness? Your Observer Self can help you discern when you should be guided by you emotions and when you should allow them to come and go without reacting to them. When you begin to examine your emotions, you realize that they naturally come and go; they are constantly changing. You can learn to tap that central idea of the Observer Self especially when you are feeling very stressed or depressed and are convinced that you will feel this way forever.

This does not mean that some people have significant levels of depression or anxiety that need to be addressed at a higher level. It also doesn't mean you should not spend time listening

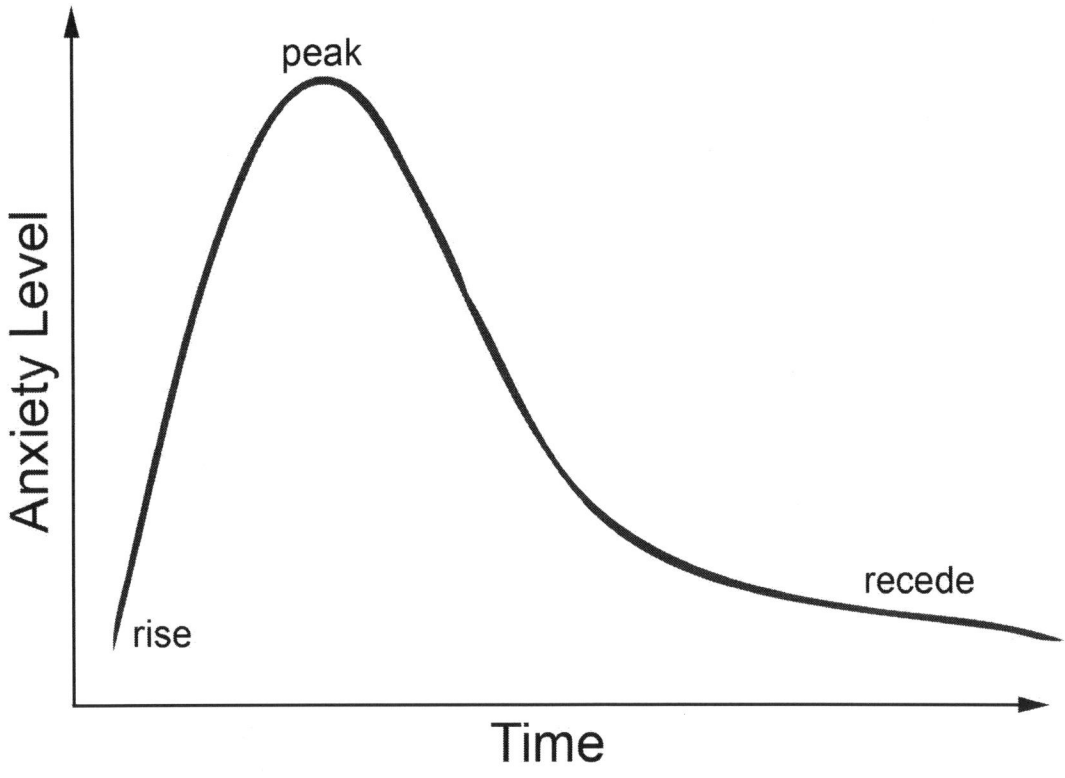

Figure 2. Emotions Come & Go: Mapping Anxiety Over Time.

to your emotions and using them to guide your actions. Instead, it means that even when you feel intense emotions, they are fluctuating, and you can learn ways to help decrease their intensity. You can better explore your emotions when you are not overwhelmed by them. Being mindful of your emotions means staying present with them without reacting or becoming enmeshed with them.

Figure 2 depicts graphically the trajectory of emotions. Looking at the graphic, you can see that emotions can increase in intensity at first, but at some point, they subside, much like a wave. All emotions pass with time. So even if you feel like things will never change, that doesn't mean they won't. In Practice 1: Surfing Emotions on the next page and Practice 2: Hand on Heart that follows, we explore how those emotions come and go, and how you can deal with them the same way: as something passing rather than fixed and unchanging.

Anatomy & Physiology: Emotions from Bottom Up or Top Down

One of the main ways our bodies help our brains determine what emotions to feel is through the **vagus nerve**. The vagus nerve is like a tree with roots; that is, it works from the bottom up, touching on most of our internal organs, including the abdomen and heart (see Figure 3). The roots continuously send signals from the organs to our brain stem, where the vagus nerve connects to the brain. In fact, 80 percent to 90 percent of the signals in the vagus flow from the body to the brain and not from the brain to the body.[6]

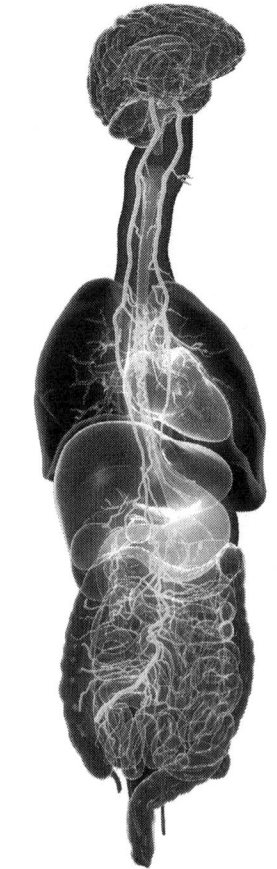

What this all means for our emotions is that our bodies actually have a lot to do with how we feel. If you ever experienced butterflies in your stomach or have a gut feeling about someone, it is a sign your vagus nerve is at work.[7] When your body feels physically healthy, the vagus sends signals to your brain that all is well, and you feel happy.

The vagus also happens to be the main way your parasympathetic nervous system exerts control over your body. In Chapter 3 Relationship with Breath, you learned that the parasympathetic nervous system helps slow you down, like the brakes in a car. The vagus is thus largely responsible for helping your heart and organs slow down.

The health of your nervous system plays a vital role in your ability to regulate your emotions. Emotions have the potential to wreak havoc on your nervous system. Being stuck in fear,

Figure 3. The vagus nerve is like a tree with roots, touching on most of our internal organs.

Practice 1: Surfing Emotions

- Take a moment to sit quietly, closing your eyes if you feel comfortable doing so, or leaving them open if you prefer. Move your attention inward.

- Notice any sensation you feel inside that feels like an emotion. It may be heat, a vibration, or a fluttering. You may not feel anything at all. Just take a moment to observe what you may feel.

- If any emotion comes up, try to stay with it, observing its quality. Where is it? Is it big or small? Does it change?

- You can imagine standing on top of it as it gets intense, and then surfing down as it lessens.

- Keep watching your emotions and noticing what comes up and when they change.

- If any emotion feels overwhelming, it's OK to open your eyes and refocus attention to something in the room or to a pleasant memory.

REFLECTING ON THE PRACTICE

Take a moment:

- Where did you feel or notice your emotions in your body?

- Did the emotions come and go in intensity?

WRAP-UP ON THE PRACTICE

Sometimes it feels as if we are stuck in an emotion and it will never end. We want to develop an awareness instead that emotions are always in flux, and that emotions and events in our life can change at any moment. All emotions pass with time. This is especially helpful during difficult times.

Practice 2: Hand on Heart

The following practice is a technique to understand how to use bottom-up processing to calm emotions. Though there is little research on this particular exercise, we know that touch is a powerful tool to release stress-relieving hormones. Many of the bottom-up practices we describe are derived from somatic therapies developed by Peter Levine, and have been shown to be beneficial for post-traumatic stress disorder (PTSD) and other stress-related issues.[8] One great thing about this exercise is that it is easy to use any time, even when you are out in public.

- Put your right hand over your heart for a few moments. You can keep your eyes open or closed. Notice any changes in your emotions or how your body feels.

- Now switch hands and put your left hand on your heart for a few moments. Again, notice any changes in your emotions or how your body feels.

- Now let's switch back and forth one more time with each hand. Put your right hand over your heart, wait a few seconds, and then put your left hand over your heart.

REFLECTING ON THE PRACTICE

Take a moment:

- Did putting a hand on your heart make you feel any calmer?

- Did one hand feel different than the other?

- What are some examples of bottom-up regulation techniques you already do? (For example, taking a shower, getting a hug, fidgeting, walking in nature, or exercising.)

anger, or anxiety can keep your sympathetic system on "go" all the time, continuously releasing hormones that tell you things are not OK. Other emotions, like joy, awe, and calm, allow the parasympathetic nervous system to come into play and slow things down, allowing your body to rest and restore.

Keeping balanced requires understanding of how to take care of your emotions. You can influence the health of your vagus nerve through mindfulness activities and exercise. This helps you to regulate your emotions. You can calm yourself by telling yourself calm thoughts, or by calming your body in a hot bath, or doing gentle stretches. Understanding the two-way street of your vagus nerve helps you understand that you can regulate your emotions top down or bottom up.

Any healthy relationship includes acceptance, compassion, and good communication. By examining your emotions with curiosity rather than avoiding them, you can understand more clearly how to relate to them.

Wrap-Up

In this chapter we explored these ideas:

• Your Observer Self can help you increase your awareness of the relationship between thoughts, emotions, and the level of a problem.

• When you are more aware that emotions can be a 4 but that the problem may be a 1, you can better calm yourself and respond to a situation.

• Daniel J. Siegel often uses the phrase "Name It to Tame It" to describe the regulating effect that merely identifying the feeling can have on the nervous system.

• Research has found that identifying and labeling the intensity of an emotion as an intervention helps calm the nervous system.

• Research has found that touch is a powerful tool to release stress-relieving hormones.

We don't need to fear or avoid emotions. Instead, we can have a healthy relationship with emotions and communicate our needs effectively. Living in reaction to every emotion leaves us feeling out of control, whereas living with our emotions, and getting to know them, better allows us to listen and respond with skill. The ability to regulate emotions is critical to good communication.

Mindfulness helps us realize that emotions are forms of communication and can be used wisely. Used wisely, both anger and love have both changed the world for the better. Knowledge that emotions are always changing can help increase your ability to get through hard times.

Chapter 5

Relationship with Thoughts

Don't believe everything you think.

Key Mental Health Concepts

- Conditioning

- Self-Talk

- Self-Compassion Versus Self-Judgment

- Common Humanity Versus Isolation

- Mindfulness Versus Overidentification

- Flexible Thinking

- Neural Pathways and Neuroplasticity

Are You Your Thoughts?

The saying at the beginning of the chapter suggests you are much more than your thoughts. That is not to say your ability to think isn't miraculous. But we've all experienced times when, on the one hand, our mind can be our biggest enemy, and then on the other, our best friend. Our relationship with our thoughts greatly influences our health and wellbeing. And getting stuck in our thoughts keeps us from living in the present moment. This chapter explores what it means to develop a healthy relationship with thoughts.

Healthy Versus Unhealthy Relationship with Thoughts

Take a moment to imagine biting into a slice of lemon. Anything happen? Often, just thinking about that bite into a lemon will prompt the body to produce extra saliva.

Then there's that snake scenario we mentioned earlier: What happens when you think about stepping on the snake? Or for some people it's remembering an encounter with a spider. The short shock to the system, the heart beating faster and the release of stress hormones, including adrenaline and cortisol, of the thought versus the event in real life can be very similar. Our bodies in these moments can't distinguish what is real and what is a thought.

Similarly, when we are enmeshed with our thoughts, we may be developing an unhealthy relationship with them, where we are creating more stress than necessary. Like when you get caught in your thoughts about a fight you had with a friend, and your body experiences the stress, as if you're there, in the argument. When you use metacognition—that is, develop an awareness of your thoughts—you can help yourself use thoughts wisely to calm or redirect yourself rather than become enmeshed or entangled in them.

Being Present Versus Being Caught in Thoughts

As therapists, we continually hear people describing their inability to "turn off their thoughts," and how much this contributes to mental health issues such as stress, depression, and trauma. Conversely, we also hear about the times they feel their best: when they are present in a moment, such as walking in nature; observing the sky, trees, and animals; petting their cat; or talking with a good friend.

Mental health involves discerning when to use thinking and when to use awareness. **"Thinking" is when our mind creates thoughts about the world or a situation we are in. "Awareness," or being present, is when our attention is focused on a situation, simply observing it with the senses**[1]—being present without analyzing or judging.

> **When you are able to distinguish where your mind is stationed—in the past, the present, or the future—you can bring your focus back to the here and now.**

If you are constantly in thinking mode, you are not fully present in a moment. Like when you find yourself lamenting or ruminating on the past, or anticipating or predicting something about the future rather than being in the here and now. Stopping thoughts altogether is never the point, nor is it even possible, but with practice, you can increasingly observe your thoughts and consciously direct your attention. Noticing how much of your time is spent thinking, planning, and reflecting, and then balancing that with time being very present—very aware—in a current moment can help reduce stress and increase mental health.

Thoughts Are Just Thoughts

A healthy relationship with thoughts begins with understanding that they are not the ultimate truth or necessarily even based on reality. Thoughts are just thoughts. And when we reside more frequently in the present, we begin to see that the mind is continually chattering away with commentary and judgment that may or may not be true. Just as we can be distracted by things in our environment—like the internet or the ticking of the clock in a room—and can't tune them out, we can also be distracted by a multitude of thoughts in our heads! Think for a moment about some of the unhelpful advice you've gotten from your thoughts:

"You could never do that."
"If you take a day off, everything will fall apart."
"No one is ever going to talk to you again after that stupid comment!"

In addition, thoughts can course through your mind like a continually looping commentary:

"What a nice day. ... I wonder if it will rain? ... I need to clean the gutters before it rains. If I don't, they'll get clogged and the rain will flow over and be really loud. And then I won't be able to sleep. ... I haven't slept well for days. I wonder how long a person can go without sleep? I'll google that. ..."

It can be reassuring to know that this stream of inner talk is common. We all have lots of thoughts. Everyone has corners of their mind that can produce wild, uncomfortable, or fearful thoughts. Everyone *also* has the capacity to focus on thoughts of serenity, good times, and happiness. Your Observer Self—introduced in Chapter 2 Relationship with the Observer Self (see p. 23)—can help you recognize your thoughts, direct your attention to a point of focus, and then use your thoughts wisely.

The Monsters on the Bus

Imagine the mind is a TV with a remote control, and you can practice changing the channels. Some people's minds are better at using attention to change the channels than others, but for most anyone, mindfulness-based mental health practices can help strengthen this ability.

Acceptance and commitment therapy (ACT), described in Chapter 2 (see p. 25), is an evidence-based therapy approach developed to help increase this psychological flexibility and awareness. One way ACT helps highlight a healthy and unhealthy relationship with thoughts is with the metaphor of monsters on a bus.

In this metaphor, life is like a bus, and you are the driver. There are monsters on the bus along for the ride, and they represent your thoughts and emotions. They yell things like:

"You are never going to make it."
"You suck!"
"This is too scary to do."
"Everyone hates you."
"You need to eat that cake."

If you listen to these monster passengers, you can forget that your Observer Self is actually in control of the bus, and then never get anywhere. Conversely, if you accept that you are always going to have thoughts and emotions giving you messages, you can listen to them without necessarily doing what they say. You can make that speech, even though you are scared, or push through fear-based thoughts to accomplish your goals. You can still drive the bus—even with loud and bossy passengers—and use the Observer Self to focus your attention on your goal rather than on them! As you learn to watch the stories you tell yourself, rather than react to them, you develop more equanimity and calm.

Let's begin with a practice that helps observe thoughts without getting caught in them.

CHAPTER 5: LET'S PRACTICE

Practice 1: Thoughts as Clouds

This activity helps you move in and out of your thoughts. This can be extremely helpful when you are consumed by rumination.

If you feel comfortable, close your eyes. This may make it easier to focus. But if you feel more comfortable with your eyes open, gently gaze at an object in front of you.

- Using your Observer Self, notice your breathing. There's no need to change anything. Just watch the inhale and exhale.

- Now imagine it is a warm, sunny day, and you're lying on your back on the soft, cool grass. Looking up, you see clouds gently drifting by in the sky. You might even notice the color of the clouds and the different shapes. Take a moment to imagine these soft fluffy clouds floating by above you.

- Now let other thoughts come into your mind.

- What does your mind think about when you let it wander? Spend a few seconds watching thoughts that come into your mind.

- See if you can notice how the thoughts are constantly changing, coming and going like clouds in the sky. It might help to imagine each thought as a cloud and watch them drift by.

(PRACTICE 1 continued on next page)

(PRACTICE 1 continued from previous page)

- If you notice that your mind is wandering or is getting stuck on a thought, good job noticing! That's your Observer Self checking in. Gently bring yourself back to the image of thoughts floating by.

- Now shift your attention back to your breath.

- Slowly open your eyes if they were closed and bring your attention back into the room.

REFLECTING ON THE PRACTICE

Take a moment to consider:

- What was it like to imagine your thoughts as clouds?.

- Did you notice certain types of thoughts that keep coming back? Worry thoughts? Planning? Thoughts that were sticky and wouldn't go away?

- Was the practice difficult or easy?.

Conditioning

Max had been unhappy at their job for years, and wanted to try something new. But every time they looked at job listings, their mind would start to spin, and they would think, "So many people are looking for jobs—they'll never hire me. Who would want someone who's been doing the same thing for 10 years? There's no point in trying."

For many people, their thoughts are controlling or defining them when they don't need to be. We are often unaware of how many of our thoughts and beliefs are automatic or conditioned, and are controlling our behavior and choices. These become the stories we unconsciously tell ourselves without questioning where they came from or if they are true.

Conditioning is a process where a thought or behavior is reinforced by a consequence. A classic example is the work of Ivan Pavlov, who trained dogs to drool at the sound of a bell after pairing the bell with their food repeatedly. This experiment shows how prone we are to conditioned responses. When we have conditioned thoughts, we may automatically think something based on a cue. Our cues can be the time of day, the drive home from work, or it can be the repetitive messages we get from TV.

Conditioning isn't necessarily good or bad. Conditioning can sometimes be helpful.

For example, if we work out at the same time each day, our bodies and minds will become conditioned to that routine, helping us get out the door. Or a warm, nurturing teacher in childhood may have helped us think positive thoughts about ourselves. When we are unaware of the process of conditioning, we may believe we cannot learn a new language because we got a bad grade in Spanish, or that we should not play the drums because of continual societal messaging that "girls don't play drums," when in reality, neither of these are true. With heightened awareness, we can use the conditioning process to help our mental health instead of aggravating it.

Instead of letting conditioned thinking go unexamined, or reacting from a conditioned or automatic pattern, you can notice exactly what is happening in a moment with a fresh lens. Just like with emotions, being more granular with your thought processes can help you increase your self-awareness and emotional intelligence. This will be part of our practice.

The following are example thought patterns described in cognitive behavioral therapy (CBT) that sometimes keep us from thinking flexibly, being in the moment, and keeping perspective.[2]

- **Black-and-white thinking** (dichotomous thinking): Focusing on the extremes; all or nothing: "I answered one question poorly in the interview—I'll never get the job."

- **Catastrophizing**: Taking every thought to the worst-case scenario—"Everything is going to fall apart."

- **Overgeneralization**: Using "always," "never," "every time," and "everybody."

- **Mental filter**: Filtering the positive from a context and keeping the negative.

- **Mind reading**: Assuming we know what others are thinking without asking.

- **Personalization**: Taking things personally when they may not have much to do with us (e.g., a friend didn't call, so they don't like us).

- **Rumination**: Having a thought or story stuck on replay over and over; also known as sticky thoughts.

- **Internalizing** racism and unconscious bias, a subconscious belief, assumption, or attitude about others that influences spot judgments and behaviors toward them.

CBT is based on the idea that emotions are difficult to change directly, but we can sometimes change how we feel by changing what we do or how we think.[3] According to CBT theory, our interpretation of what is happening, not what objectively is happening, affects our emotions.

Self-Talk & Self-Compassion

Another way our thoughts can affect our health and wellbeing relates to our **self-talk**. Becoming more aware of the things we tell ourselves is an important skill because the way we

Cognitive Behavioral Therapy, Mindfulness-Based Cognitive Behavioral Therapy, and Mindfulness-Based Stress Reduction

Cognitive behavioral therapy (CBT) is a form of psychological treatment that has been demonstrated to be effective for a range of problems including depression, anxiety disorders, alcohol and drug use problems, marital problems, eating disorders, and severe mental illness. CBT focuses on understanding thinking patterns, becoming more aware of learned patterns of unhelpful thinking and behavior, and identifying alternate ways of thinking.

Mindfulness-based CBT (MBCBT)[4] is a version of CBT based on Jon Kabat-Zinn's work called Mindfulness-based Stress Reduction (MBSR)[5] that brings present moment awareness and compassion into the practices. MBSR has been studied extensively, and uses meditation, yoga, and self-inquiry to help people change their relationship to stress and everyday life.

talk to ourselves directly affects how we feel. For example, being critical of ourselves is associated with increased depression and anxiety.[6-8] On the other hand, treating ourselves with compassion can increase our wellbeing and help us stay within our emotional Window of Tolerance.[9] (For a review of the Window of Tolerance, see p. 9).

Psychologist Kristin Neff researches the effects of self-compassion on wellbeing. She describes three components of self-compassion.[10]

• The first is **self-compassion versus self-judgment**, which means learning to meet challenges and disappointing experiences with kindness toward ourselves rather than harsh criticism. Being able to do so leads to feeling calmer and more centered overall.

• The second factor is **common humanity versus isolation**. This means recognizing we are not alone in our suffering. In fact, suffering is something all humans have in common, and we can connect with each other through our suffering. Dr. Neff states, "Therefore, self-compassion involves recognizing that suffering and personal inadequacy is part of the shared human experience—something that we all go through rather than being something that happens to "me" alone.

  • The third factor she identifies is **mindfulness versus overidentification**. She says that self-compassion requires taking a balanced approach to our negative emotions so that feelings are neither suppressed nor exaggerated. This is the slight distance we can get from intense thoughts or emotions when we use our Observer Self, rather than getting enmeshed with them and having zero larger perspective.

This concept of mindfulness versus overidentification refers to what we discussed in our last chapter on emotions—that being aware of and naming emotions helps us develop a healthy relationship with emotions, as opposed to being enmeshed with them. We have found that most of us are unconscious of how harsh we are with ourselves. When asked, most people don't have language for self-compassion.

Often, people worry that showing compassion toward themselves and others will decrease motivation to accomplish their goals or get through difficult tasks. Dr. Neff's research actually finds the opposite: People who display more compassion toward themselves increase resilience and motivation in the face of failure.[11] It may feel really odd to be so kind to yourself and others if you are used to using competition and harshness to motivate, but research from the Gottman Institute reveals that the "magic ratio" for a healthy marriage is 5-to-1, meaning five positives to one negative interaction! It makes sense that when developing a healthy relationship with yourself, you would want a similar ratio.

CHAPTER 5: LET'S PRACTICE (MORE)

Practice 2: Increasing Self-Compassion

The following is an exercise from Dr. Neff's website:[12]

1. If we ask the question, "How would you treat a friend," first, think about a time when a close friend felt bad about themselves or felt they failed in some way. How did you respond to your friend in this situation? Please write down what you typically do, and what you say, and note the tone in which you typically talk to your friends.

2. Now think about times when you felt bad about yourself or felt you failed. How did you respond to yourself in this situation? Please write down what you typically do, and what you say, and note the tone in which you talk to yourself.

(PRACTICE 2 continued on next page)

(PRACTICE 2 continued from previous page)

3. Did you notice a difference? If so, ask yourself, why? What factors or fears come into play that led you to treat yourself and others so differently?

4. Please write down how you think things might change if you responded to yourself in the same way you typically respond to a close friend when you're suffering.

On reflection, the question then becomes: **Why not try treat yourself like you would a good friend and see what happens?**

Rigid Versus Flexible Thinking

Often, when we are angry or scared, our thinking becomes more rigid. We ruminate about the same thought and have difficulty seeing multiple perspectives. When we begin to move outside our emotional Window of Tolerance, our thoughts either get more rigid or more chaotic.

For example, when we are being observed by our boss, we may be less likely to be creative, spontaneous, and relatable during a presentation, and instead plod through reading the content nervously, like a robot. Robot brain takes over creative and flexible brain. We often see people who get angry and get stuck on one thought for hours after feeling "dissed," thinking over and over, "I hate so-and-so!" or "That was so unfair!" And it repeats. Replaying takes over flexible thinking. Until the emotion settles, it is difficult for our perspective to broaden.

The good news is that as you increase your cognitive flexibly, you often decrease stress. Noticing whether you are in flexible mode or rigid mode can help you increase self-awareness and emotional regulation. Taking mindful moments and using the practices and activities in this workbook can help you notice when you get stuck on replay or have a very narrow "I am right" perspective, and check in to see if you think more flexibly.

A Taoist Fable of Maybe

There is a Taoist story that helps exemplify the narrow reactive mindset versus a more open and integrated perspective. It goes like this:

> There once was an old farmer who had worked his crops for many years. One day his horse ran away. Upon hearing the news, his neighbors came to visit. "Such bad luck," they said, sympathetically.

"Maybe," the farmer replied.

The next morning the horse returned, bringing with it three other wild horses. "How wonderful," the neighbors exclaimed.

"Maybe," replied the old man.

The following day, his son tried to ride one of the untamed horses, was thrown, and broke his leg. The neighbors again came to offer their sympathy on his misfortune.

"Maybe," answered the farmer.

The day after, military officials came to the village to draft young men into the army. Seeing that the son's leg was broken, they passed him by. The neighbors congratulated the farmer on how well things had turned out.

"Maybe," said the farmer.

Think about a time when you were in a situation that seemed "bad" but turned out much differently than expected, or even turned out to be a "good" thing in the end. Most successful people have found that what they thought were failures were stepping stones to learning and growing.

Anatomy & Physiology: Neural Pathways: What Fires Together Wires Together

In Chapter 1 Mental Health & Mindfulness, we introduced the idea of neuroplasticity, the brain's ability to continually grow and change as long as we are alive. How the brain changes depends mainly on our experiences, which activate neurons, the brain's nerve cells. When a neuron gets activated, it "fires," causing an electrical signal to travel down the length of its body, the axon (seen in Figure 1), to the end of the neuron, the axon terminals. The axon terminals then release a chemical message that crosses a small gap that separates the neurons called the synapse. The message is received by the next neuron's dendrites, creating a connection.

Each time we learn something new, the brain creates a memory for it in the form of new connections of neurons that fire together. These intricate connections are called **neural pathways**. The saying "Cells that wire together, fire together" was coined by neuroscientist Carla Shatz to paraphrase what is also known as Hebb's Law.[13]

For example, when you learn a new piece on the piano, that information is stored in the brain in the form of these neuronal connections or a new pathway. These connections can grow stronger with repeated practice, like making a small path into a well-paved road.

Other ways the brain adapts to learning is through growing new neurons and increasing

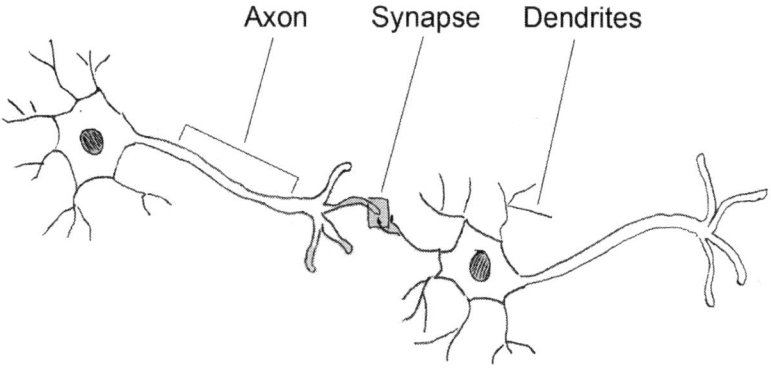

Axon   Synapse   Dendrites

Figure 1. Synapse Between Two Neurons of the Brain

the speed at which existing neurons can fire. This is called **neuroplasticity**, which explains how our minds are conditioned to respond to situations automatically in the same pattern. When we repeatedly practice the same responses, they get strongly wired into the brain.

We can think of neuroplasticity as akin to building train tracks. When we learn something new, we create a track for it that runs from point A to point B. The track gets greased each time we use it, allowing the train to go faster. If we want to learn to get to point B a different way, or if we want to go to another place altogether, point C, then we have to make the effort to lay down a new track.

We also need to be mindful about practicing, using the new track instead of the easier old one. In this way, we help shape our brains by becoming more aware of our behaviors and thought patterns, and how they are shaping the structures of our brains.

Gratitude & Mental Health

By using our attention wisely, we can affect the development of neural pathways in our brains. When we focus on looking for threats in our environment, we get better at finding threats. On the other hand, if we are practicing a gratitude meditation every evening before bed, we are strengthening the pathways that help us feel grateful.

Research indicates that practicing gratitude regularly has a variety of benefits for physical and mental health, including helping us feel happier,[14,15] decreasing stress,[16,17] and improving our relationships.[18,19] Expressing gratitude toward a friend or partner actually helps you feel closer to them.[19]

Evidence suggests that gratitude and appreciation contribute to workplaces where employees actually want to come to work and don't feel like cogs in a machine.[20] As previously mentioned, individuals tend to have a greater awareness of the challenges they encounter, commonly referred to as "headwinds," rather than recognizing the advantages they enjoy, known as "tailwinds."[21] However, research indicates that focusing on the positive, or having gratitude, helps to reframe our mindset, amplify positive experiences, build resilience, and strengthen social connections, all of which contribute to enhancing positive emotions and overall wellbeing.[15]

It is essential to note that gratitude isn't one-size-fits-all, but a very individualized practice. In addition, it does not mean always "looking on the bright side," which can lead to ignoring real problems. Instead, gratitude seems to help establish balance when the brain can be hijacked by the negative. Practicing gratitude helps you notice the little wins, like sweet moments with children that can often get overshadowed by the intense headlines or problems at work; or getting a recipe right after several tries; or shaving a few seconds off your personal best race time.

CHAPTER 5: LET'S PRACTICE (EVEN MORE)

Practice 3: Gratitude Journal

This practice is based on three concepts: What we think affects how we feel; how we feel affects how we think, and we can have more control over our attention.

THE PRACTICE

- Take a minute to get settled. Move your focus from outside to inside.

- Now think of five things you are grateful for.

- Take a few minutes to write down each one, allowing ample time to think in detail about each thing.

- Notice how you feel.

REFLECTION ON THE PRACTICE

- What happened to your thoughts?

- Were you able to keep your focus on thoughts about being grateful?

Wrap-Up

In this chapter, we learned that, if we are unaware of our thought patterns, thoughts can pull us into the past or future without our noticing. By using mindfulness practices, you can become a better observer of where your mind is stationed, and practice staying in the present more often. You can also take moments to reflect with awareness on things you're grateful for, no matter how small, to develop neural pathways that sustain wellbeing and satisfaction with life.

We also learned that we can identify and label our thoughts to help us notice thought patterns and conditioned behavior. By using your Observer Self, you can choose which thoughts you attend to, and which ones you might want to let float by.

In all those ways, you develop a healthy relationship between your thoughts and feelings. You can have intense thoughts—and you don't need to react to them; you can instead respond to them wisely. You can develop the ability to shift attention to and from your thoughts with more ease, to better follow your deepest values.

CHAPTER 5: FINAL PRACTICE

Practice 4: Noticing Your Thoughts

This week, practice noticing your thoughts. Just watch them, and notice any stories you tell yourself that may or may not be true.

Chapter 6

Relationship with the Body

*A compassionate, healthy relationship with the body
is essential to mental health.*

Key Mental Health Concepts

- Top-Down and Bottom-Up Processing

- Body Image

- Underidentification and Overidentification with the Body

- Thin Ideal

- Health at Every Size

- Interoception

- Weight Stigma

Our Bodies & Mental Health

The body carries us through life. It's no wonder that research links taking care of our bodies to mental health, emotional regulation, and wellbeing. To be healthy, our bodies need a balance of exertion and rest. Exercising as little as 30 minutes a day, three days a week, can be as effective as medication in the treatment of mild to moderate anxiety and depression.[1] Dr. Michael Craig Miller from Harvard Medical School states, "In people who are depressed, neuroscientists have noticed that the hippocampus in the brain—the region that helps regulate mood—is smaller. Exercise supports nerve cell growth in the hippocampus, improving nerve cell connections, which helps relieve depression."[2]

Research also shows that moderately intensive exercise and a well-balanced diet improve brain function, contributing to a better working memory and the ability to think flexibly[3-5] And increasingly, research finds that exercise can help emotional resilience—our ability to handle day-to-day setbacks and adversity. By stressing our physical muscles regularly, we increase the capacity of our emotional "muscle," or our Window of Tolerance—"we can change how we respond to stress" through physical activity.[6]

The brain and body need exercise for mental health, and they also need rest. The combination of regular exercise, which activates the sympathetic part of our nervous system, and regular rest and relaxation, which activates the sympathetic or rest and digest system, keeps our nervous system balanced.

During the sleep cycle, the human brain undergoes various stages of rest in different regions of the brain. Within these stages, the brain performs crucial tasks such as the assessment and consolidation of thoughts and memories. Insufficient sleep negatively impacts this process. The REM (rapid eye movement) sleep phase plays a fundamental role in the processing of emotional information by the brain, and is particularly essential for functions such as memory, learning, and creativity. Additionally, delta sleep, also known as deep sleep, significantly contributes to brain function, memory, and metabolism—all functions of our body that reduce fatigue when attended to. When you rest, your body naturally reduces the levels of cortisol and other stress hormones. Well-rested people have been shown to stay calmer and react less strongly to negative situations.[7]

With all the influence rest and exercise have on mental health, we take the time in this last chapter to look at the interconnection between thoughts, emotions, and the body. Rather than explore how to take care of your body from the outside in, like how to change how you look, we explore how to care for your body from the inside out. We begin to explore how stress, trauma, and cultural pressures influence your relationship with your body and how to stay in your Window of Tolerance by listening to and accepting your body. We explore science-backed activities that show us how listening to our bodies can guide us to better health.

We know that trauma and chronic stress dysregulate the nervous system. By reimagining your relationship with exercise, rest, and food, you can find meaningful and enjoyable ways for taking care of your mental and physical health.

How Your Body Helps You Stay Healthy

Too often we see the body as an enemy, and we frame self-care as taking care of our bodies; however, your body can also take care of you! Your body signals when you are hungry, thirsty, tired, full, excited, angry, and in love. Your body can inform you that you need to establish a boundary, reduce your stress, or stretch out your muscles. The question then becomes, how do you listen to your body to stay emotionally regulated and healthy?

As discussed in earlier chapters, **top-down processing** refers to using the mind, or thinking differently, to influence how we behave and feel. Many of the skills practiced up to this point use top-down techniques, such as observing thoughts and emotions; comparing the level of a problem to the intensity of emotional response; and engaging in compassionate self-talk. Sometimes this is really hard to do, and you may need some other strategies, ones that are not mind-based, but body-based.

Many people, when asked what they do to take care of stress, report body-based strategies like exercise, walking in nature, sinking into a hot bath, or petting their cats. These types of practices affect our bodies, which then send signals of calm to the brain. We call this **bottom-up processing**, which includes diaphragmatic breathing, the reaction of our bodies to heat or cold, and listening to music. These activities change our nervous systems without us having to "try," by changing how we think, and they can automatically affect our nervous system when incorporated into our everyday routines.

Bottom-up processing uses the body to change how we think and feel—changing our thoughts and emotions by using our bodies as tools for self-regulation. In a healthy relationship with the body, we utilize both coping methods—top-down and bottom-up processing—developing kind and compassionate inner conversations with and about the body, as well as a deep understanding of bodily strategies that calm our nervous system when we are stressed. Having all of these options helps us stay more often in our Window of Tolerance.

Healthy emotional relationships, in general, rely on mutual respect, trust, support, and good communication—and a sense of playfulness always helps. In the face of unrealistic expectations of perfection or performance, these relationships suffer. Our relationship with our body is no different; it requires compassion, care, knowledge, and encouragement to develop sustainable habits of self-care. Conversely, having unrealistic expectations for our bodies can lead to unhealthy relationships with exercise and food as well as poor mental health. If we blame, ignore, or live in a state of constant disappointment, it's hard to maintain a caring or accepting attitude. **We usually don't take care of things we don't like or appreciate.**

Are You Your Body?

Picture yourself as a baby, then when you were five and fifteen, and now. You look quite different at every age. Realizing this can help us have a more flexible and realistic relationship with our bodies and selves as we go through various stages of change. And, once again, we can call upon the Observer Self to help us get there. As was true in our exploration in previous chapters of the breath, emotions, and thoughts, you can use the Observer Self to help develop a healthier relationship with your body throughout your life.

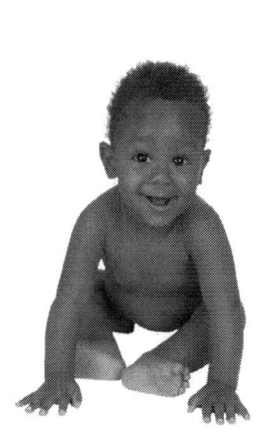

We know accepting body-based change can be very difficult. In the dominant U.S. culture and in many other cultures where a prevailing belief is that our bodies define our worth, or where there is a narrow version of beauty, it can be hard to accept all the aspects of the body we were born with—for instance, our height, weight, physical ability, hair color and texture, facial features, and skin tone.

In many cultures, our bodies and how they appear, or their abilities, are often viewed as problems or deficient. Social media, television, film, and magazines all constantly promote images of ideal body types and ways of looking that are unrealistic for most of us.

However, we are starting to see signs that values and beliefs are shifting as acceptance increases of gender identities, age-related changes, and diverse body types. Recent research finds, for instance, that weight is a lesser indicator of health than previously thought. According to Dr. Nichole Kelly, a professor at the University of Oregon, "society fixates on weight as the main measure of fitness, despite the fact that eating habits, exercise, and sleep are all better predictors of health. Feeling a lack of social support is a better predictor of premature morbidity and mortality than weight. How do we help people feel more supported and less alone? I just think we are misdirected in our efforts to help people be healthier and happier."[8]

Underidentification & Overidentification

Two key concepts that we can use to guide the Observer Self in developing a healthier relationship with the body are underidentification and overidentification.

Underidentification shows up as a neglectful relationship with our bodies, where even basic needs are ignored. This may happen because we are too busy, or because we feel shame about our body. When we underidentify with the body, we operate as though our bodies are the enemy and ignore its needs for rest, exercise, and healthy eating. For example, drinking a caffeine-loaded cup (or two) of coffee to continuously force wakefulness instead of setting a regular sleep schedule; ignoring hunger because of being too busy to eat; or the opposite, ignoring feeling full.

On the other hand, **overidentification** may present itself as being overly concerned with looks, giving looks uppermost importance in how you feel about yourself or function day to day. For example, not going to a party because your hair came out "wrong" or you feel "fat." When our identities are overly wrapped up in how we look or what is going on with our bodies, our identity becomes too enmeshed with our bodies. Our mood, behavior, and sense of wellbeing is dependent on appearing or functioning in a certain way. We may observe this clearly in others— like we absolutely don't care or think any less of a friend when their hair is messy, or they gain or lose a few pounds. But for ourselves, those situations may challenge us to the point that we lose sight of who we are at a deeper level.

Underidentifying and overidentifying with the body are coping mechanisms in response to uncomfortable feelings about the body or its changes. When our reaction is to underidentify, there is too little focus, or we avoid thinking about it. When we overidentify, we have too much focus on our body; we may try to excessively control it.

Practice 1: Underidentification & Overidentification

- Think of times when you underidentified with your body and ignored its cues. Can you think of two or three examples? Write them down.

- Now think of a time you overidentified with your body, paying too much attention to it. What are some examples you can think of? Write those down.

REFLECTION ON THE PRACTICE

- How might underidentifying and overidentifying negatively affect your health and wellbeing, and in the examples you wrote down?

- How do you think what we see in the media affects body image and self-talk, and in the examples you wrote down?

Listening to the Body—The Power of Interoception

We all have a friend or family member whose mood completely depends on the mood of their partner: If their partner is upset, they are equally upset. If their partner is depressed, they become depressed. The emotional boundaries between the two people are unclear. **And with no healthy boundaries, it is very difficult to have a healthy relationship.**

The relationship with our body and our thoughts and emotions that we discussed in previous chapters is no different. We can become too close, or enmeshed, to see the separation clearly. For example, sometimes we look at a cake and think, "Wow, that looks good. I could eat the entire thing." In those kinds of situations, we are listening to a thought or emotion rather than actual hunger cues. In the same way, we may lie on the couch binge-watching TV when we are sluggish, misunderstanding the body's cue that it instead needs to get moving.

It's understandable why these situations happen, but in general, bodies don't like being tired, overly full, stagnant, or hungry. With practice, we can get better at noticing the difference between cues our body is sending versus thoughts and feelings. (Some research suggests that the dieting cycle of gaining and losing weight can inhibit the body's ability to feel satiated after eating. Therefore, for those who cannot tune into hunger cues, a healthy relationship with body and food may be related more to understanding healthy intake and nutrition than listening to the body.[9])

We can use our Observer Self, for instance, to eat with more attunement, or notice we are tired, and not lazy, and take a rest. We can tune into the way our body and mind react when we get hungry, full, or anxious. In this way, we develop a compassionate and empathetic relationship with our body, and use the body to focus attention and respond to self-care needs such as hunger, rest, or movement.

This kind of physiological awareness and regulation is called **interoception**. Interoception is a crucial skill for stress reduction, self-management, mental and emotional wellbeing, and learning. It is important in the development of positive or negative body image and the development of lifelong beliefs and habits related to the body and exercise.[10]

We understand that developing a healthy relationship with the body is neither easy nor instantaneous. There are many very real physical, emotional, cultural, and time-related challenges. But by finding ways to begin to focus attention on interoception and other mindfulness-based practices, over time, you can reshape your relationship with your body to one of cooperation and care. That's what we explore in the rest of this chapter.

What Keeps Us from a Healthy Relationship with Our Bodies?

The Thin Ideal

The dominant messages in the United States about how to relate to our bodies are quite convoluted. Very few of us come into adulthood with a healthy **body image**. And no wonder. From a very early age, we receive messages about how a body should look. Children's books, toys, and cartoons all send tacit messages about the ideal body. As adults, we continue to absorb these messages from the media every day. These messages typically reinforce what is called the **thin ideal**: the notion that the thinner the body, the better—that thinness leads to better health, more success, and happiness.[11,12] The thin ideal fuels **weight stigma** by lending it social acceptability. (See section below for more information about weight stigma.)

We as humans are not supposed to all look alike. And rather than focusing on the behaviors that create overall health in individuals—such as healthy eating, exercise, and emotional regulation—the thin ideal of the dominant culture instead encourages people to focus on appearance and thinness as an indicator of health and success.

In reality, we know that people who are thin and look "good" can be very unhealthy and have an unhealthy relationship with the body that includes calorie restriction, poor nutrition, and body hatred.[13] And people who have larger bodies can be and often are very healthy. Research shows that adhering to the thin ideal can have detrimental effects on health and wellbeing, including increased body-focused anxiety, negative emotions, and poor self-esteem.[14-16] Importantly, these unrealistic pressures inhibit a trusting relationship with the body. Media and consumerism support a goal of zero fat and dieting, and encourage perfectionism instead of embracing and promoting the natural diversity of body types and the habits that are good health indicators of every body type. One approach that has gained recognition in recent years is **Health at Every Size**®, developed by Linda Bacon, PhD, which supports the perspective that wellbeing and healthy habits are more important than body weight.[17]

Weight Stigma

Adding to the dominant message of the thin ideal is weight stigma, which devalues people who do not fit into prevailing societal norms for weight, body shape, and size.[18] Weight discrimination is pervasive in our culture, but may often go unrecognized because it is deemed a socially acceptable form of bias.[19,20]

As with other forms of discrimination, weight stigma carries detrimental physical and mental health-related consequences for the people who are its target, including heightened mortality, heightened levels of substance use, and increased risk for depression and anxiety.[21-23] Weight-based stereotypes that larger-bodied people are lazy, have poor willpower, and are unattractive give way to prejudice and systemic discrimination in the workplace, education, health care, and at fitness centers.

Although some believe that applying social pressure to lose weight can be effective, Yale health researchers Rebecca Puhl and Chelsea Heuer state that weight stigma is "not a beneficial public health tool for reducing obesity. Rather, stigmatization of obese individuals threatens health, generates health disparities, and interferes with effective obesity intervention efforts."[20]

Actively countering discriminatory weight- and body-related messages and beliefs can help remediate the negative health effects of fat shaming. Teaching healthy behaviors, while celebrating the natural diversity in body size and shape, is essential to changing the current culture toward health and wellbeing for all.

Weight, the Dieting Myth & Body Acceptance

Counter to what most people believe, research supports the fact that focusing on weight does not actually encourage people to lose weight or adopt healthy habits. As a result, the majority of people who diet to lose weight are unable to maintain the weight loss over the long term, and often even gain weight.[24,25]

Body acceptance helps empower people to take care of themselves as they are, developing healthy, attainable lifestyle habits. Importantly, this acceptance of diversity in body size and shape has shown to increase health-positive behaviors. Having realistic expectations and body acceptance brings us into our Window of Tolerance, increasing emotional stability and embodiment over dissociation from the body, making us more likely to make healthy life decisions. Promoting this kind of culture of health can help improve mental and physical health and decrease shaming, bullying, and judgment about body size.[26]

Practice 2: Body Image & Self-Compassion/Self-Talk

As we noticed in Chapter 5 Relationship with Thoughts, we are often very hard on ourselves without realizing it. How we talk to ourselves makes a big difference in our mental health, which includes the conversations we have with our bodies. How often do you hear someone actually appreciating their body?

"Thank you, feet, for getting me where I need to go all day!"

"Wow, totally amazing that I can hike up this hill or run or walk a mile!"

The first may seem farfetched, but the second? That's pure, personal appreciation for what your body can do. Instead, for many of us, our self-talk focuses on the negative, what we don't like about our looks rather than the opposite—what looks or feels good.

Bodies do a lot for us, and being thoughtful about how we relate to our bodies can make the difference between being healthy and energized, or being stressed and depressed. Appreciating and getting to know our bodies with curiosity helps us take good care through each stage of life.

THE PRACTICE

Take some time to think about the following questions:

- Do you talk to or about your body like you would to a good friend?

- What belief or beliefs underlie how you relate to your body?

- How do you take care of your body (e.g., food, exercise, rest, and relaxation)?

- Now fill in a Window of Tolerance worksheet (see p. 17) with a few body-based activities that help you feel better.

Anatomy & Physiology: The Enteric Nervous System

In previous chapters, we saw that the body is constantly communicating information up to the brain through the vagus nerve. In this chapter, we explore how, because of this bottom-up communication, we can use the body to regulate our emotions. As mentioned previously, these body-based (bottom-up) practices that use our senses can often be less effortful and produce more immediate change than top-down (cognitive-based) practices such as self-talk.

In this section, we want to highlight another part of the nervous system that is intricately related to the vagus nerve and bottom-up regulation—the enteric nervous system (ENS). Like the vagus nerve, the ENS is integral to sending information from the body to the brain. Understanding how the ENS works can help us navigate mental health in new ways.

The ENS, often referred to as the second brain or the gut-brain axis, is responsible for digestion, and recent studies have found that the digestive system has major implications for mental and emotional health. We all know that anxiety can affect digestion and that people who are stressed often complain about stomach aches. The ENS is largely responsible for these symptoms. The ENS is composed of two thin layers of more than 100 million nerve cells lining your gastrointestinal tract, from the esophagus to the rectum. It is mostly independent of the central nervous system, and is generally regulated by the sympathetic and parasympathetic parts of the nervous system, which we discussed in Chapter 3 Relationship with Breath. In that chapter, we learned that while the sympathetic nervous system is the gas pedal, the parasympathetic nervous system (PNS) constitutes the brakes—and is responsible for helping us relax by slowing down our heartbeat and lowering our blood pressure. The PNS is also helpful in getting us into rest and digestion modes, and it does this by activating the ENS.

> The enteric nervous system is important for mental and emotional health. It can trigger emotional shifts by sending signals to the brain.

When we are in a relaxed state, the PNS stimulates the enteric function, enhancing digestion. Alternately, the sympathetic nervous system inhibits enteric function. This is why, when we are stressed, we may get stomach aches or not be able to eat. When we relax, our ENS is activated, and nutrients and neurotransmitters flow more freely through the body. Digestion involves a complex series of hormonal signals between the gut and the nervous system, and it seems to take about 20 minutes for the brain to register satiety (fullness). If someone eats too quickly, satiety may occur after overeating instead of putting a stop to it. There's also reason to believe that eating while we're distracted by activities like driving or typing may slow down or stop digestion in a manner similar to how the "fight or flight" response does. And if we're not digesting well, we may be missing out on the full nutritive value of some of the food we're consuming. For all of these reasons, digestion has a large influence over our mood.

Beyond its nutritional function, the ENS is also important for mental and emotional health. It can trigger emotional shifts by sending signals to the brain through neurotransmitters. These neurotransmitters play a critical role in maintaining both homeostasis (a stable equilibrium) and chronic stress in the body. Dr. Jay Pasricha of Johns Hopkins University says that researchers and doctors thought that anxiety and depression contributed to problems like bloating, diarrhea, constipation, irritable bowel syndrome, and pain. But new studies are finding that that it may also be *the other way around*: Irritation in the gut may be responsible for sending neurotransmitters to the brain that trigger anxiety or depression.[27] (See Figure 1.)

For example, the ENS uses more than 30 neurotransmitters, many identical to those in the brain, such as acetylcholine, dopamine, and serotonin. (Neurotransmitters are chemical messengers that carry signals from nerve cells [neurons] to other nerve cells, muscle cells, or glands.) In fact, more than **90% of the body's serotonin (which influences learning, memory, and happiness, and regulates hunger among other things)** and about **50% of the body's dopamine** (a chemical in the brain that makes you feel good) are located in the gut! With that information, we can see why taking care of our gut is essential to mental and emotional health for so many reasons.

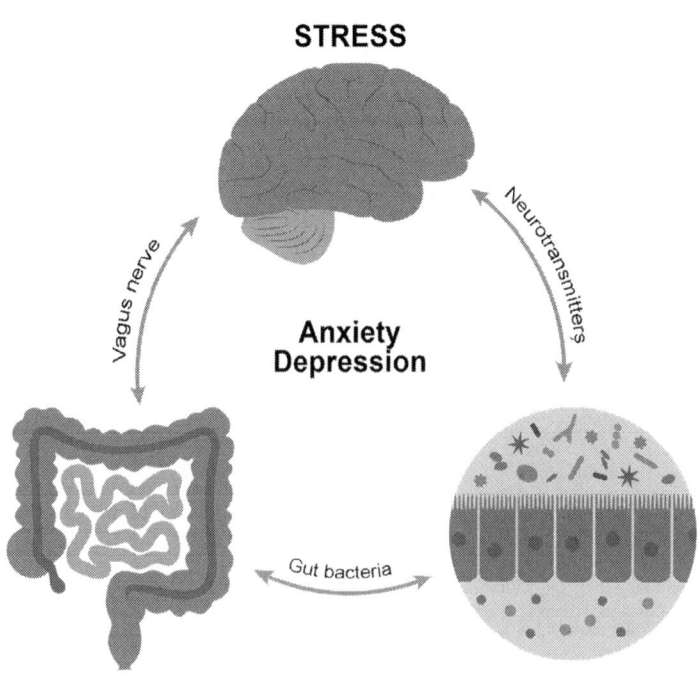

Figure 1. The gut affects mental health, sending neurotransmitters that can trigger anxiety and depression.

The Practice of Mindful Eating

In Chapter 2 Relationship with the Observer Self, we introduced a practice to mindful eating to focus attention and build awareness. We can expand on the ideas introduced there by identifying approaches to mindful eating, which include:

- Taking note of emotionally eating when not hungry.

- Eating slowly and really tasting food (remember, it takes 20 minutes to register fullness).

- Filling up to full rather than overly full.

- Incorporating satiating foods into diets to reduce cravings, such as bananas, yogurt, cheese, avocados, nuts, and beans.

- Noticing how the things you eat affect how you feel (energized, lethargic).

Other approaches can include creating routines, just like with exercise, that may help decrease food-based decision fatigue or mindless eating. And then there is portion size and specifically identifying foods that make you feel energized and satisfied, as part of learning what works for you and your mind and body. Some people eat smaller amounts throughout the day, and some eat three satiating meals and don't snack in between.

Taking the time to find your unique relationship and your routines with food is not easy, but can lead to lifelong benefits in both your mental and physical health.

Finding Physical, Mental & Emotional Balance Through Body-Based Practices: Exercise for Mental Health

Just like our relationship to food, our values and beliefs about exercise can influence our ability to use it for our mental health. Developing a compassionate relationship with movement and exercise goes beyond losing weight or getting toned. **Movement can help us to regulate our nervous systems, and we can also use movement and the body to focus attention and relieve the mind. We can use movement to upregulate or downregulate our nervous systems.** By doing more vigorous exercise, we may be able to increase energy and help depression. By doing more restorative practices like walking in nature and stretching, we can rejuvenate and calm anxiety. Lifting weights or dancing might help us when we are feeling down, and stretching or swimming might help our anxiety.

In addition, exercise or movement can be used as a mindfulness tool to anchor our attention. For example, when you go out to shoot hoops or take a hip-hop class, you focus your attention on the movement and your body in an active way, helping bring you into the present moment with full attention. You may notice that part of the appeal of focused exercise or movement is that it pauses or redirects the incessant worry and rumination going on in your head.

So, we can think of exercise as a way to stay emotionally regulated and healthy. Imagine if we all responded to stress by saying, "I need to go for a walk!" Not only would we all be more physically healthy, but we would probably have better relationships and better overall mental health by maintaining our Window of Tolerance—because exercising releases chemicals in our bodies that actually calm us down and increase our ability to think clearly.

Pause for Reflection

We know that most people don't get enough exercise even though they know that it helps their health and wellbeing. Why do you think this is? Some possibilities include:

- We can be harsh with ourselves sometimes, and that affects our mood and motivation.

- We get caught in shaming thoughts. Notice the difference between saying to yourself "You better go exercise or you will get fat!" versus "Go exercise because it will make you feel better." How different does that feel?

- We get caught judging ourselves about our body's ability to move or exercise. Ironically, our thoughts about exercise are often hindering us from reaping the mental health benefits of it!

- We tend to think that all people need to exercise in the same way or be athletic, which can impact our motivation. If we think we need to go out and run three miles or do an hour of hard-core workouts every day, we may just throw in the towel before we get started. But actually, people can be very healthy by walking, dancing, gardening, and even cleaning their houses. Non-athletic people can be active and healthy, and many people may not like traditional sports.

Instead of being hard on yourself to get motivated to move and stay healthy, research shows that self-compassion increases healthy behaviors and motivation, and can decrease symptoms of anxiety and depression.[28]

Movement to Increase Calm & Focus: The Balancing Effect of Yoga

We can use movement to help give us more energy, calm us down, or focus our attention and increase our awareness of what is going on in our bodies and mind, or with our emotions. Certain types of activities are especially helpful to increasing calm and focus. **Embodying activities are those that increase our awareness of how the body feels and functions in a way that increases self-confidence.**

Yoga in particular has been found to help improve body image and decrease self-criticism of the body. Many people think of yoga as exercise, but yoga is really a moving meditation, where the body is used as a tool to help us remain very present in the moment with our internal conversations and sensations. In one study, teens were assigned to either a yoga class or their usual physical education (PE) class.[29] After 12 weeks, the students in yoga were found to spend less time worrying about their physical appearance than the students in the regular PE group. They also appreciated their bodies more and expressed more positive body image. These effects were especially strong for girls. Other studies have shown that yoga may help support a positive body image and increase interoception, or the awareness of the physiological state of the body.[30,31]

Below, we begin to explore yoga to develop more body awareness from the inside out. **The word "yoga" actually means "union," and practicing yoga can help create a healthy balance between relaxation and exercise, and mind and body.** Through yoga, we can explore ways to activate the parasympathetic nervous system when we are stressed, or ways to activate the sympathetic nervous system if we are depressed, to help us come back into balance. In yoga, this balance is achieved by moving between relaxation and exertion regularly so that your nervous system remains balanced. Many yoga sequences move from an activating pose to a relaxing pose. Just like with regular exercise, we need to rest our muscles after a workout to allow them to heal. Practices that alternate between rest and exertion activate the vagus nerve, which signals our body to relax and de-stress.

Ideally, each individual is able to create practices that help them deal with stress appropriately so they don't get stuck in perpetual stress mode. It is important to note that everyone's body is different, and what is healthy for one person may not be for another. Getting to know your own body and the physical activities that make you feel healthy is a foundation of yoga practice.

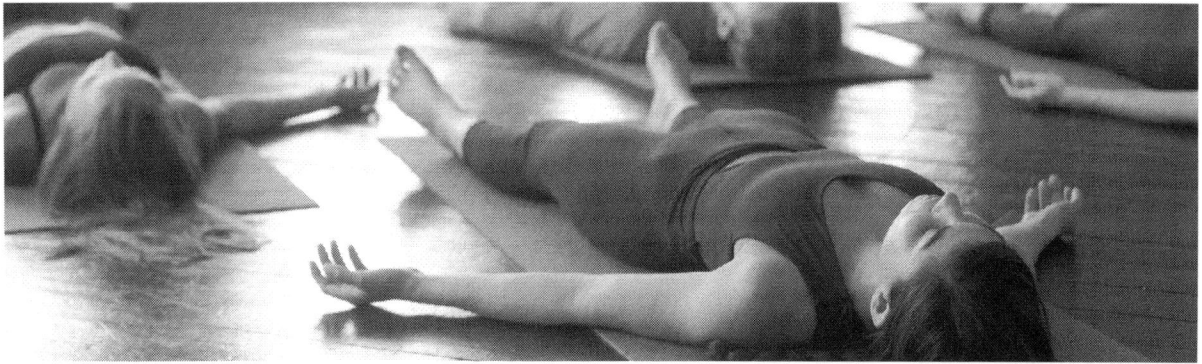

What follows is a series of yoga practices to tap during your everyday activities, to focus attention and downregulate the nervous system.

Practice 3: Mindful Movement—Forward Bend

- Stand up or stay seated and begin by grounding your feet, feeling them solid on the floor.

- Inhale and slowly raise your arms up over your head, looking up at your hands.

- Exhale and slowly lower your hands down as you bend forward. Exhale all the way.

- Now, take two deep, long breaths in this pose.

- After, your second breath, gently inhale and begin to rise, arms overhead.

- Exhale as you bring your arms down by your side.

Practice 4: Mindful Movement—Gentle Twist

- Take a moment to settle into your chair or sit up straight on a mat.

- Again, use your breath to turn your attention from outer to inner observing.

- Pushing down into the floor or seat, notice your spine rising.

- Slowly begin to twist to the right, using your arms to gently assist the movement until you feel a natural stopping point. No painful or intense movement should be used.

- Now take three deep, long breaths, inhaling through the nose and exhaling through the nose.

- After the third breath, gently unwind.

- Repeat on your other side.

Practice 5: Mindful Movement—Gentle Back Bend

- Now let's try another mindful movement.

- Again, sit up tall in your seat.

- Bring your hands over your head and clasp your hands behind your head.

- Plant your feet at on the floor and feel the solidness of the ground beneath your feet.

- Arch your upper back into your hands slightly, opening up your chest area and expanding your shoulders down toward your back.

- Take 3 deep long breaths.

- Let your body come back to sitting and lower your arms back down by your side.

- Notice how you feel in this pose.

- Notice if you feel more or less tension or anxiety.

- Notice the quality of your breath.

- Notice any effects on emotions or thoughts.

REFLECTION ON THE PRACTICE

- Did that brief mindful movement sequence affect your Window of Tolerance or sense of calm? Did it make you more or less anxious?

- What about the movements themselves: Were there movements you liked better than others? Did some movements affect your mood differently than others? For example, did one feel more calming or energizing than another?

- Did some movements affect your mood differently than others? For example, did one feel more calming or energizing than another?

By checking in, we can discover what movements work best for our individual bodies and minds.

Practice 6: Guided Relaxation to Balance the Nervous System

As we discussed above, rest and relaxation are just as important as exercise and good nutrition. Our bodies, minds, and emotions need rest. Rest allows our bodies to recover from a workout; specifically, workouts deplete glycogen stores in the muscles leading to muscle fatigue, and rest replenishes them, allowing our muscles to repair and restore energy. Therefore, it is important to take time to let our bodies integrate the effects of a workout, sometimes taking a few days off from lifting or running.

Similarly, we need to take time to integrate emotional experiences. Emotional exhaustion is different from the physical exhaustion of a workout,[32] but requires the same attention to rest. Rest and relaxation help us maintain mental clarity and emotional balance. It is helpful to take time to rest after intense emotional experiences and integrate our nervous systems after emotionally or mentally challenging times. This allows emotional experiences to integrate into our brains and bodies over being stuck in rumination or overwhelm. Remember, our bodies can't really distinguish when we are experiencing a real threat or when we are rehashing a stressful event. Stress hormones rush through our bodies even after an event if we can't disengage our thinking from and return to the present moment.

In yoga, there is a practice called Shavasana, the Sanskrit name for a restorative pose that ends the yoga practice with you lying on the ground resting, the whole body completely relaxed, allowing the body to integrate the practice. We recommend doing a variation of Shavasana throughout the day whenever possible, taking time after intense meetings or hard conversations to just sit (or find floor space to lie down, if possible) and allow the body and mind to integrate the experience. As we get better at listening and communicating compassionately with our bodies, we will notice that to be healthy, our bodies require a balance between exercise and rest.

The following is a short practice to support finding relaxation when you can find some space on a floor.

(PRACTICE 6 continued on next page)

(PRACTICE 6 continued from previous page)

- Take a moment to find a comfortable position lying on your back on the floor.

- Sit comfortably, and if you feel comfortable doing so, close your eyes very softly and very gently; or leave your eyes open, if you prefer.

- Let's begin with the toes: Wiggle your toes; now feel them relax.

- Relax your ankles and feet. Feel your feet heavy and completely relaxed.

- Move your attention to your shins and calves. Feel the weight of the bones and muscles sinking toward the ground as you allow the muscles around them to rest.

- Move up toward your thighs. If thoughts come up that are judgmental or distracting, just notice and let them go.

- Continue to focus on your legs, noticing any tension and consciously letting it go.

- Move to focusing on your hips . . . then your stomach . . . and your waist, encouraging your organs inside to relax and sink back toward your spine.

- Relax your back. From the top to the bottom, the entire back is relaxed, feeling your spine spread and release.

- Relax your chest . . . and shoulders. Feel your shoulders melting into the floor below.

- Relax your upper arms.

- Relax each muscle in your forearms . . . your hands . . . right up to your fingertips.

- Relax the neck muscles.

- Move your awareness up to your face. Relax the jaws . . . mouth . . . nose . . . eyes . . . earlobes . . . facial muscles . . . forehead . . . all the way to the top of your head. Lie still and quietly for a few moments.

- Slowly roll to one side and come up to a seated position.

(PRACTICE 6 continued on next page)

(PRACTICE 6 continued from previous page)

- Now take a deep breath and begin to wiggle your fingers and toes.

- Slowly roll to one side and come up to a seated position.

REFLECTION ON THE PRACTICE

- How did this meditation make you feel?

- What barriers or beliefs get in the way of you resting or getting enough movement into your day?

- Do you have a good balance between rest and relaxation and exercise?

- What are ways you get rest throughout the day?

- How do you get exercise, and what are ways for you incorporate movement into your everyday?

Wrap-Up

As we become more aware of how our values and beliefs about bodies influence our mental health, we can help shift our relationship with our body and learn to not only accept diverse body types, gender identities, and age-related changes, but to appreciate our bodies through all of its stages. Having unrealistic expectations, or being overidentified or underidentified with our bodies, decreases our health behaviors and takes our time and attention away from our deeper values.

A healthy body image means we can accept, appreciate, and respect our body. This is not the same as body satisfaction, as you can be dissatisfied with aspects of your body, yet still be able to accept it for all its limitations. Good communication with the body and compassionate self-talk support us in taking better care of ourselves. The goal of a mindful relationship is to treat yourself and your body as you would a dear friend.

Finally, we can use the body to focus our attention; we can use activity to interrupt rumination. And movement can be a bottom-up intervention, directly affecting our nervous system. In an activity using progressive muscle relaxation, we practice focusing the mind and relaxing the body. We may notice areas where we hold tension and be able to release. We may notice areas where we are able to completely relax and use this feeling to help other areas relax. With practice, we can use this activity to deactivate the stress response and help our bodies come back to homeostasis and heal.

Either way, we can learn to use movement and rest for better mental health.

Remember:

- Be kind and compassionate to your body as a form of care.

- Balance rest and relaxation with exercise for good health.

- Take time to get to know your body's needs. Everyone is different.

- Try to listen carefully to your body's signals.

- Notice when you are hungry, tired, or need exercise.

- Think about what you do each day to care for your body from the inside out.

- Have realistic expectations and body acceptance to support staying in your Window of Tolerance, which increases emotional stability and embodiment rather than dissociation from the body.

References

Introduction

1. World Health Organization. (2023). *Mental health* [Fact sheet]. https://www.who.int/en/newsroom/fact-sheets/detail/mental-health-strengthening-our-response

2. attune. (2019). En.OxfordDictionaries.com. https://en.oxforddictionaries.com/definition/attune

3. Niles, A. N., & O'Donovan, A. (2018). Anxiety and depression symptoms comparable to obesity and smoking as prospective predictors of major medical illnesses and somatic symptoms. *Health Psychology*, *38(2)*, 172-181.

4. Levine, P. A. (1997). *Waking the tiger: Healing trauma: The innate capacity to transform overwhelming experiences*. North Atlantic Books.

5. Corso, P. S., Edwards, V. J., Fang, X., & Mercy, J. A. (2008). Health-related quality of life among adults who experienced maltreatment during childhood. *American Journal of Public Health*, *98*, 1094-1100.

6. Chapman, D. P., Anda, R. F., Felitti, V. J., Dube, S. R., Edwards, V. J., & Whitfield, C. L. (2004). Adverse childhood experiences and the risk of depressive disorders in adulthood. *Journal of Affect Disorders*, *82*, 217-225.

7. Sacks, V., Murphey, D., & Moore, K. (2014). Adverse Childhood Experiences—National and state-level prevalence. https://www.childtrends.org/publications/adverse-childhood-experiences-national-and-state-level-prevalence

8. Richards, T. N., Schwartz, J. A., & Wright, E. (2021). Examining adverse childhood experiences among Native American persons in a nationally representative sample: Differences among racial/ethnic groups and race/ethnicity-sex dyads. *Child Abuse & Neglect*, *111*. https://doi.org/10.1016/j.chiabu.2020.104812

9. Tang, S. S. (2023). *Asian American psychology and psychotherapy: Intergenerational trauma, betrayal, and liberation*. Rowman & Littlefield.

10. Ortiz, R., & Sibinga, E. M. (2017). The role of mindfulness in reducing the adverse effects of childhood stress and trauma. *Children (Basel, Switzerland)*, *4(3)*, 16. https://doi.org/10.3390/children4030016.

11. Mikolajczak, M. (2014). The impact of emotional intelligence on physical health. *Personality and Individual Differences*, *60*, S22. https://doi.org/10.1016/j.paid.2013.07.404.

12. Gottman, J., & Schwartz Gottman, J. (2015). *Emotion coaching: The heart of parenting*. The Gottman Institute.

Chapter 1: Mental Health & Mindfulness

1. World Health Organization. (2023). *Mental health* [Fact sheet]. https://www.who.int/en/news-room/fact-sheets/detail/mental-health-strengthening-our-response

2. Siegel, D. J. (2010). *The mindful therapist: A clinician's guide to mindsight and neural integration*. W.W. Norton & Company, Inc.

3. Siegel, D. J. (2018). *Aware: The science and practice of presence*. TarcherPerigee.

4. Neff, K. D., & Germer, C. (2017). Self-compassion and psychological wellbeing. In J. Doty (Ed.) *Oxford handbook of compassion science*, Ch. 27. Oxford University Press.

5. Herculano-Houzel, S. (2009). The human brain in numbers: A linearly scaled-up primate brain. *Frontiers in Human Neuroscience*, *3*, 31. https://doi.org/10.3389/neuro.09.031.2009

6. Kang, D. H., Jo, H. J., Jung, W. H., Kim, S. H., Jung, Y. H., Choi, C. H., ... Kwon, J. S. (2012). The effect of meditation on brain structure: cortical thickness mapping and diffusion tensor imaging. *Social Cognitive and Affective Neuroscience*, *8(1)*, 27–33. https://doi.org/10.1093/scan/nss056

7. Lazar, S. W., Kerr, C. E., Wasserman, R. H., Gray, J. R., Greve, D. N., Treadway, M. T., ... Fischl, B. (2005). Meditation experience is associated with increased cortical thickness. *Neuroreport*, *16(17)*, 1893-1897.

8. Hölzel, B. K., Carmody, J., Vangel, M., Congleton, C., Yerramsetti, S. M., Gard, T., & Lazar, S. W. (2010). Mindfulness practice leads to increases in regional brain gray matter density. *Psychiatry Research*, *191(1)*, 36-43. https://doi.org/10.1016/j.pscychresns.2010.08.006

Chapter 2: Relationship with the Observer Self

1. Linehan, M. M. (2015). *DBT® skills training manual (2nd ed.)*. Guilford Press.

2. Hayes, S. C, Strosahl, K. D., & Wilson, K. G. (2012). *Acceptance and commitment therapy: The process and practice of mindful change (2nd ed.)*. Guilford Press.

3. Bishop, S., Duncan, J., Brett, M., & Lawrence, A. D. (2007). Prefrontal cortical function and anxiety: Controlling attention to threat-related stimuli. *Nature Neuroscience, 7*, 184-188.

4. Siegel, D. J. (2010). *Mindsight: The new science of personal transformation.* Bantam Books.

5. Siegel, D. J. (2018). *Aware: The science and practice of presence.* TarcherPerigee.

Chapter 3: Relationship with Breath

1. Gerritsen, R. J. S., & Band, G. P. H. (2018). Breath of life: The respiratory vagal stimulation model of contemplative activity. *Frontiers in Human Neuroscience, 12*, Article ID 397. https://doi.org/10.3389/fnhum.2018.00397

2. Russo, M. A., Santarelli, D. M., & O'Rourke, D. (2017). The physiological effects of slow breathing in the healthy human. *Breathe, 13(4)*, 298-309. https://doi.org/10.1183/20734735.009817

3. Tang, Y.-Y., Hölzel, B. K., & Posner, M. I. (2015). The neuroscience of mindfulness meditation. *Nature Reviews Neuroscience, 16(4)*, 213-225. https://doi.org/10.1038/nrn3916

4. Jha, A. P., Krompinger, J., & Baime, M. J. (2007). Mindfulness training modifies subsystems of attention. *Cognitive, Affective & Behavioral Neuroscience, 7*, 109. https://doi.org/10.3758/CABN.7.2.109

5. Lutz, A., Slagter, H. A., Dunne, J. D., & Davidson, R. J. (2008). Attention regulation and monitoring in meditation. *Trends in Cognitive Sciences, 12(4)*, 163-169. https://doi.org/10.1016/j.tics.2008.01.005

6. Creswell, J. D., & Lindsay, E. K. (2014). How does mindfulness training affect health? A mindfulness stress buffering account. *Current Directions in Psychological Science, 23(6)*, 401-407. https://doi.org/10.1177/0963721414547415

7. Tang, Y-Y., Ma Y., Fan Y., Feng, H., Junhong, W., Feng., S., Lu, Q., Hu, B., Lin, Y., Li, J., Zhang, Y., Wang, Y., Zhou, L. & Fan, M. (2009). Central and autonomic nervous system interaction is altered by short-term meditation. Proceedings of the National Academy of Sciences of the United States of America, *106(22)*, 8865-70. https://doi.org/10.1073/pnas.0904031106

8. Azam, M. A., Katz, J., Mohabir, V., & Ritvo, P. (2016). Individuals with tension and migraine headaches exhibit increased heart rate variability during post-stress mindfulness meditation practice but a decrease during a post-stress control condition—A randomized, controlled experiment. *International Journal of Psychophysiology, 110*, 66-74. https://doi.org/10.1016/j.ijpsycho.2016.10.011

9. Burg, J. M., Wolf, O. T., & Michalak, J. (2012). Mindfulness as self-regulated attention: Associations with heart rate variability. *Swiss Journal of Psychology*, 71(3), 135-139. https://doi.org/10.1024/1421-0185/a000080

10. Chambers, R., Lo, B. C. Y., & Allen, N. B. (2008). The impact of intensive mindfulness training on attentional control, cognitive style, and affect. *Cognitive Therapy Research*, *32*, 91, 303-322.

11. Tang, Y. Y., Tang, R., & Posner, M. I. (2014). Improving creativity performance by short-term meditation. *Behavior and Brain Function*, *10*, 9.

12. Linehan, M. M. (2015). *DBT® skills training manual (2nd ed.)*. Guilford Press.

Chapter 4: Relationship with Emotions

1. Barrett, L.F. (2017). *How emotions are made: The secret life of the brain*. Houghton Mifflin Harcourt.

2. Goleman, D. (1995). *Emotional intelligence*. Bantam Books.

3. Acceptance and Commitment Therapy. (2022, March 21). *Psychology Today*. https://www.psychologytoday.com/us/therapy-types/acceptance-and-commitment-therapy

4. Siegel, D. J., & Bryson, T. P. (2011). *The whole brain child*. Delacorte Press.

5. Kircanski, K., Lieberman, M. D., & Craske, M. G. (2012). Feelings into words: Contributions of language to exposure therapy. *Psychological Science*, *23(10)*, 1086–1091. https://doi.org/10.1177/0956797612443830

6. Tubbs R. S., Rizk E., Shoja M. M., Loukas M., Barbaro N., & Spinner R. J. (2015). Nerves and nerve injuries: *Vol 1: History, embryology, anatomy, imaging, and diagnostics*. Academic Press.

7. Breit, S., Kupferberg, A., Rogler, G., & Hasler, G. (2018). Vagus nerve as modulator of the brain-gut axis in psychiatric and inflammatory disorders. *Frontiers in psychiatry*, *9*, 44. https://doi.org/10.3389/fpsyt.2018.00044

8. Kuhfuß, M., Maldei, T., Hetmanek, A., & Baumann, N. (2021). Somatic experiencing—effectiveness and key factors of a body-oriented trauma therapy: A scoping literature review. *Eur J Psychotraumatol*, *12(1)*. https://www.ncbi.nlm.nih.gov/pmc/articles/PMC8276649/

Chapter 5: Relationship with Thoughts

1. Arno. (2009, November 19). Thinking vs. Awareness. *The Warrior Way*. https://warriorsway.com/thinking-vs-awareness/

2. Burns, D. D. (1980). *Feeling good: The new mood therapy*. New American Library.

3. Cully, J. A., & Teten, A. L. (2008). *A therapist's guide to brief cognitive behavioral therapy*. Department of Veterans Affairs South Central MIRECC.

4. *What is Cognitive Behavioral Therapy?* (2017). American Psychological Assocation. https://www.apa.org/ptsd-guideline/patients-and-families/cognitive-behavioral

5. *MBSR 8-week online.* (2023). UMass Memorial Health. https://www.ummhealth.org/umass-memorial-medical-center/services-treatments/center-for-mindfulness/mindfulness-programs/mbsr-8-week-online-live

6. Ehret, A. M., Joormann, J., & Berking, M. (2015). Examining risk and resilience factors for depression: The role of self-criticism and self-compassion. *Cognition & Emotion, 29*, 1496-1504.

7. MacBeth, A., & Gumley, A. (2013). Exploring compassion: A meta-analysis of the association between self-compassion and psychopathology. *Clinical Psychology Review, 32*, 545-552.

8. Werner, K. H., Jazaieri, J., Goldin, P., Ziv, M., Heimberg, R. G., & Gross, J. J. (2012). Self-compassion and social anxiety disorder. *Anxiety, Stress & Coping: An International Journal, 25*, 543-558.

9. Leary, M. R., Tate, E. B., Adams, C. E., Allen, A. B., & Hancock, J. (2007). Self-compassion and reactions to unpleasant self-relevant events: The implications of treating oneself kindly. *Journal of Personality and Social Psychology, 92*, 887- 904.

10. Neff, K. D. (2003). The development and validation of a scale to measure self-compassion. *Self and Identity, 2*, 223-250.

11. Neff, K. D., & McGehee, P. (2010). Self-compassion and psychological resilience among adolescents and young adults. *Self and Identity, 9(3)*, 225-240. https://doi.org/10.1080/15298860902979307

12. Neff, K. D., Self-compassion: Exercise 1: How would you treat a friend. https://self-compassion.org/exercise-1-treat-friend/

13. Hebb, D. O. (1949). *The Organization of Behavior*. Wiley & Sons.

14. Watkins, P. C., McLaughlin, T., & Parker, J. P. (2021). Gratitude and subjective wellbeing: Cultivating gratitude for a harvest of happiness. *Research Anthology on Rehabilitation Practices and Therapy*, 1737-1759. IGI Global.

15. Witvliet, C. V., Richie, F. J., Root Luna, L. M., & Van Tongeren, D. R. (2019). Gratitude predicts hope and happiness: A two-study assessment of traits and states. *The Journal of Positive Psychology, 14(3)*, 271-282.

16. Jans-Beken, L., Jacobs, N., Janssens, M., Peeters, S., Reijnders, J., Lechner, L., & Lataster, J. (2020). Gratitude and health: An updated review. *The Journal of Positive Psychology, 15(6)*, 743-782.

17. O'Leary, K., & Dockray, S. (2015). The effects of two novel gratitude and mindfulness interventions on wellbeing. *The Journal of Alternative and Complementary Medicine, 21(4)*, 243-245.

18. Bartlett, M. Y., Condon, P., Cruz, J., Baumann, J., & Desteno, D. (2012). Gratitude: Prompting behaviours that build relationships. *Cognition & Emotion, 26(1)*, 2-13.

19. Lambert, N. M., Clark, M. S., Durtschi, J., Fincham, F. D., & Graham, S. M. (2010). Benefits of expressing gratitude: Expressing gratitude to a partner changes one's view of the relationship. *Psychological Science, 21(4)*, 574-580.

20. Newman, K. M. (2017, September 6). *How gratitude can transform your workplace.* Greater Good Science Center. https://greatergood.berkeley.edu/article/item/how_gratitude_can_transform_your_workplace

21. *How to practice gratitude.* (2023.) Mindful. https://www.mindful.org/an-introduction-to-mindful-gratitude

Chapter 6: Relationship with the Body

1. Pearce M., Garcia L; Abbas A., et al. (2022.) Association between physical activity and risk of depression: a systematic review and meta-analysis. *JAMA Psychiatry, 79(6)*, 550-559.

2. *Exercise is an all-natural treatment to fight depression.* (2021, February 2). Harvard Health Publishing. https://www.health.harvard.edu/mind-and-mood/exercise-is-an-all-natural-treatment-to-fight-depression

3. Sandoz, E., & DuFrene, T. (2014). *Living with your body and other things you hate: How to let go of your struggle with body image using acceptance and commitment therapy.* New Harbinger.

4. Eyre, H., Kahn, R., Robertson, R. M. & ACS/ADA/AHA Collaborative Writing Committee. (2004). Preventing cancer, cardiovascular disease, and diabetes: A common agenda for the American Cancer Society, the American Diabetes Association, and the American Heart Association. *Diabetes Care, 27(7)*, 1812-24. https://doi.org/10.2337/diacare.27.7.1812

5. Naidoo, U. (2018, December 7). *Gut feelings. How food affects your mood.* Harvard Health Publishing. https://www.health.harvard.edu/blog/gut-feelings-how-food-affects-your-mood-2018120715548

6. Soong, K. (2023, February 3). *How exercise can help you build resilience at any age.* The Washington Post. www.washingtonpost.com/wellness/2023/02/03/building-resilience-exercise-stress/

7. *How sleep deprivation impacts mental health.* (2022, March 16). Columbia Psychiatry News. https://www.columbiapsychiatry.org/news/how-sleep-deprivation-affects-your-mental-health

8. Howe Camozzi, R. (2022). College of Education Researcher: Rethink our focus on weight. *Oregon Quarterly, 101(2).*

9. Moy, J., Petrie, T. A., Dockendorff, S., Greenleaf, C., & Martin, S. (2013). Dieting, exercise, and intuitive eating among early adolescents. *Eating Behaviors, 14(4),* 529-532.

10. Voelker, D. K., Reel, J. J., & Greenleaf, C. (2015). Weight status and body image perceptions in adolescents: current perspectives. *Adolescent Health, Medicine and Therapeutics, 6,* 149-158. https://doi.org/10.2147/AHMT.S68344

11. Low, K. G.; Charanasomboon, S.; Brown, C.; Hiltunen, G.; Long, K.; Reinhalter, K.; Jones, H. (2003). Internalization of the thin ideal: Weight and body image concerns. *Social Behavior and Personality: An International Journal, 31,* 81-89. https://doi.org/10.2224/sbp.2003.31.1.81

12. McCarthy M. (1990.) The thin ideal, depression and eating disorders in women. *Behav Res Ther, 28(3),* 205–215.

13. Hawkins, N.; Richards, P. S.; Granley, H. M. C.; Stein, D. M. (2004). The Impact of Exposure to the Thin-Ideal Media Image on Women. *Eating Disorders, 12(1),* 35-50. https://doi.org/10.1080/10640260490267751

14. Brown, A., & Dittmar, H. (2005). Think "thin" and feel bad: The role of appearance schema activation, attention level, and thin–ideal internalization for young women's responses to ultra–thin media ideals. *Journal of Social and Clinical Psychology, 24(8),* 1088-1113. https://doi.org/10.1521/jscp.2005.24.8.1088

15. Harper, B., & Tiggemann, M. (2008). The effect of thin ideal media images on women's self-objectification, mood, and body image. *Sex Roles, 58,* 649. https://doi.org/10.1007/s111 99-007-9379-x

16. Pidgeon, A., & Harker, R. A. (2013). Body-focused anxiety in women: Associations with internalization of the thin-ideal, dieting frequency, body mass index and media effects. *Open Journal of Medical Psychology, 2(4B),* 17-24. https://doi.org/10.4236/ojmp.2013.24B004

17. Robison J. (2005). Health at every size: Toward a new paradigm of weight and health. *MedGenMed : Medscape general medicine, 7(3)*, 13.

18. Tomiyama, A. J., Carr, D., Granberg, E. M., Major, B., Robinson, E., Sutin, A. R., & Brewis, A. (2018). How and why weight stigma drives the obesity 'epidemic' and harms health. *BMC medicine, 16(1)*, 123. https://doi.org/10.1186/s12916-018-1116-5

19. Puhl R. M., & Heuer, C. A. (2009). The stigma of obesity: a review and update. *Obesity, 17(5)*, 941-964. https://doi.org/10.1038/oby.2008.636

20. Puhl, R. M., & Heuer, C. A. (2010). Obesity stigma: important considerations for public health. *American Journal of Public Health, 100(6)*, 1019-1028. https://doi.org/10.2105/AJPH.2009.15949

21. Sutin, A.R., Stephan, Y., & Terracciano, A. (2015). Weight discrimination and risk of mortality. *Psychological Science, 26(11)*, 1803-11. https://doi.org/10.1177/0956797615601103

22. Hatzenbuehler, M. L., Keyes, K. M., & Hasin, D. S. (2009). Associations between perceived weight discrimination and the prevalence of psychiatric disorders in the general population. *Obesity, 17(11)*, 2033-2039. https://doi.org/10.1038/oby.2009.131

23. Borrell, L .N., Jacobs, D. R., Williams, D. R., Pletcher, M. J., Houston, T. K., & Kiefe, C. I. (2007). Self-reported racial discrimination and substance use in the coronary artery risk development in adults study. *American Journal of Epidemiology*, 166(9), 1068-1079.

24. Mann, T., Tomiyama, A. J., Westling, E., Lew, A. M., Samuels, B., & Chatman, J. (2007). Medicare's search for effective obesity treatments: diets are not the answer. *The American Psychologist, 62(3)*, 220-33.

25. Neumark-Sztainer, D., Wall, M., Story, M., & Standish, A.R. (2012). Dieting and unhealthy weight control behaviors during adolescence: Associations with 10-year changes in body mass index. *Journal of Adolescent Health, 50(1)*, 80-86. https://doi.org/10.1016/j.jadohealth.2011.05.010

26. Sandoz, E., & DuFrene, T. (2014). *Living with your body and other things you hate: How to let go of your struggle with body image using Acceptance and Commitment Therapy*. New Harbinger.

27. *The Brain-Gut Connection*. Johns Hopkins Medicine. https://www.hopkinsmedicine.org/health/wellness-and-prevention/the-brain-gut-connection

28. Schooler, D. (2008). Real women have curves a longitudinal investigation of TV and the body image development of Latina adolescents. *J. Adolesc.*, *23*, 132–153. https://doi.org/10.1177/0743558407310712

29. Menzel, J. E., & Levine, M. P. (2011). Embodying experiences and the promotion of positive body image: The example of competitive athletics. In R. M. Calagero, S. Tantleff-Dunn, J. K. Thompson (Eds.), *Self-objectification in women: Causes, consequences, and counteractions* (pp. 163-186). American Psychological Association.

30. Villemure, C., Čeko, M., Cotton, V. A., & Bushnell, M. C. (2010). Insular cortex mediates increased pain tolerance in yoga practitioners. *Cerebral Cortex*, *24(10)*, 2732–2740. https://doi.org/10.1093/cercor/bht124

31. Mahlo, L., & Tiggemann, M. (2016). Yoga and positive body image: A test of the Embodiment Model. *Body Image*, *18*, 135-142. https://doi.org/10.1016/j.bodyim.2016.06.008

32. Hülsheger, U., Alberts, H., Feinholdt, A., & Lang, J. (2012.) Benefits of mindfulness at work: the role of mindfulness in emotion regulation, emotional exhaustion, and job satisfaction. *J Appl Psychol.*, *98(2)*. https://doi.org/10.1037/a0031313

Made in the USA
Columbia, SC
19 March 2025

55358199R00059